PEN AMERICA

Published by PEN American Center,
an affiliate of International PEN,
the worldwide association of writers
working to advance literature
and defend free expression.

www.pen.org/journal

PEN America: A Journal for Writers and Readers
Issue 13: Lovers

PEN American Center
588 Broadway, Suite 303
New York, NY 10012

This issue is made possible by the generous funding of The Lillian Goldman Charitable Trust.

Printed in the United States of America by McNaughton and Gunn.

Postmaster: Send address changes to *PEN AMERICA*, c/o PEN American Center, 588 Broadway, Suite 303, New York, NY 10012.

Email: journal@pen.org
Phone: (212) 334 1660 ext. 115

Cover art: *Couple*, by Daisy Rockwell, aka Lapata (2010). Acrylic on wooden panel.

ISBN: 0-934638-31-4
ISSN: 1536-0261

PEN AMERICA

13 | Lovers

EDITOR
M Mark

MANAGING EDITOR
David Haglund

ASSISTANT EDITORS
Sara Crosby, A.N. Devers, Matthew Goodman,
Seán Michael Leahy, Loren Noveck, Elsbeth Pancrazi,
Tommy Rudnick, Eli Spindel

LAYOUT/ART EDITOR
Justin Goldberg

INTERNS
Callie Beusman, Casey Gonzalez, Leily Kleinbard, Alexandra Wong

ADVISORY BOARD
Patricia Bosworth, Thulani Davis, Lynn Goldberg, Amy P. Goldman,
Neil Gordon, Jessica Hagedorn, Robert Kelly, Ann Lauterbach, Phillip Lopate,
Albert Mobilio, Honor Moore, Laurie Muchnick, Geoffrey O'Brien,
Ann Patty, Robert Polito, Elaine Showalter

JOIN US!

BECOME A MEMBER
OF THE FRIENDS OF *PEN AMERICA*.

PEN America is published with the help of PEN Members and a generous grant from the Lillian Goldman Charitable Trust. We also depend on the support of our readers. This publication would not be possible without help from the supporters listed on the next page.

Since 2001, we have provided a home for literature that speaks across cultural, political, and linguistic boundaries. Please join us in this important work.

If you are able, consider supporting us at one of the following levels:

FRIEND: $100-$249
Friends receive a book by one of our contributors and acknowledgment in every issue of the journal for a full year and on our website.

ALLY: $250-$499
Allies receive a signed book by one of our contributors and acknowledgment in the journal and on our website.

COMPATRIOT: $500-$999
Compatriots receive invitations to PEN events, a signed book by one of our contributors, and acknowledgment in the journal and on our website.

AMBASSADOR: $1000-$2499
Ambassadors receive invitations to PEN parties and events, a personalized book by one of our contributors, and acknowledgment in the journal and on our website.

COUNCIL: $2500+
Council members will have tea with our editor, and receive invitations to PEN parties and events, a personalized book, and acknowledgment in the journal and on our website.

Your contribution will be tax-deductible to the fullest extent allowed by law, and can be made by check or credit card. We will send you a receipt. Checks should be made payable to PEN American Center and mailed to:

PEN AMERICA JOURNAL
588 Broadway, Suite 303
New York, NY 10012

To pay by credit card please visit
www.pen.org/supportthejournal

CONTENTS

Opposite: Daisy Rockwell, aka Lapata, *Tuna Princess* (detail). Acrylic on wooden panel. In June, twenty-year-old New Jersey resident Mohamed Mahmood Alessa was arrested on the way to join a militant group in Somalia. His mother said he wanted to take his cat, Tuna Princess; she said no, and they argued.

LOVERS: A FORUM

*Tell us about a writer who is especially dear to you—
a literary mentor, forebear, friend, or lover...*

STRANGE CONNECTIONS | JESSICA HAGEDORN

Many writers have inspired me throughout my life. Strange connections: Lorca's yearning connected to my Filipino-ness and to my being a poet first. Even in translation, Lorca's musicality and haunting rhythms were and are a gift. So I guess you could call him my first love.

The spunky street-wise poems of Victor Hernández Cruz—who was my age and already published while I was still finding my voice—came next. Around the time when I also connected to Ntozake Shange, Ishmael Reed, Thulani Davis, and Miguel Piñero. Among others. You might say they taught me how to be an American. To try expanding my vision and write novels and plays. Again, I fell in love. It was the '70s: You could have more than one lover.

Which brings me to Manuel Puig and García Márquez. Cabrera Infante. Lispector. Mad love, utterly liberating. Still carry a torch for those folk.

Three years ago I stumbled upon Roberto Bolaño in a gloomy dive in Mexico City. He was by himself, nursing a drink. Reposado blanco, what else do you expect?

He asked me for a cigarette.

I thought you were dead, I said.

We've been together ever since.

DEITIES | JOHN BARTH

My chief literary navigation-stars—all first encountered in my university

undergraduate days and steered by ever since—are four: Odysseus, the arche-
typal Wandering Hero, en route home from Troy; Scheherazade, yarning
through 1001 nights to save the kingdom and her neck; Don Quixote, tilting at
windmills with his sarcastic sidekick Sancho; and Huck Finn, rafting down the
heart-waters of America. While there are numerous others that I admire, these
remain the principal deities in my pantheon.

A NEEDFUL THING | YUSEF KOMUNYAKAA

I have been greatly influenced by Robert Hayden, the man and his poetry, but
recently I argued with myself for days, wondering if I have been perhaps more
profoundly influenced by Frederick Douglass. I arm-wrestled myself, going
back and forth, and, of course, Douglass finally overpowered Hayden. When
I return to the pages Douglass amassed, his spirit prevails. Here is a man
born as a slave; his mother dies when he is only seven; he confronts the slave-
owner and the slave-breaker, educates himself, and demands to be heard. He
was not only a great observer but an acute listener—and most likely this is
why there's a pristine tonality in his language: a language of unearthing, not
obfuscation.

As a poet, I read everything aloud as I write; after thinking about the music
pulsing in Douglass's prose, I believe he also read his work aloud as he traversed
the deep night of the soul. One doesn't have to tick off this man's attributes to
realize he invented himself through a superb imagination.

Douglass portrays himself through vivid imagery. We find ourselves facing a man anointed by violence, touched by an urgency embedded in language,
moved by a dignified music. What he says is momentous, but how he says it
is momentous also, with reverence for beauty and concision. The timbre of his
voice doesn't convey a hint of sentimentality. His call is rendered through the
shape of a merciless question beckoning in the double darkness of a personal
history that still tinctures our presence. His voice is a struck bell left quivering in the metallic air lit by "a cowskin and a heavy cudgel." Ironically, I have
returned repeatedly to Hayden's "Frederick Douglass" to grasp his presence
again:

> When it is finally ours, this freedom, this liberty, this beautiful
> and terrible thing, needful to man as air,
> usable as earth; when it belongs at last to all,
> when it is truly instinct, brain matter, diastole, systole,

> reflex action; when it is finally won; when it is more
> than the gaudy mumbo jumbo of politicians:
> this man, this Douglass, this former slave, this Negro
> beaten to his knees, exiled, visioning a world
> where none is lonely, none hunted, alien,
> this man, superb in love and logic, this man
> shall be remembered. Oh, not with statues' rhetoric,
> not with legends and poems and wreaths of bronze alone,
> but with the lives grown out of his life, the lives
> fleshing his dream of the beautiful, needful thing.

Hayden's Douglass, "this man" shaped by a heroic reasoning, is for many of us a signpost. To be a true citizen is to honor what he stands for. This becomes apparent especially in "What to the Slave Is the Fourth of July?: An Address Delivered in Rochester, New York, on 5 July 1852." Returning to this piece after many years, I was surprised by the poetry in Douglass's prose—which has been measured and honed—as well as the inclusion of quotations from Longfellow's "A Psalm of Life," Garrison's "The Triumph of Freedom," Shakespeare's *Julius Caesar*, and, of course, numerous poetic Biblical references throughout. The echo of poetry guides Douglass to moments such as this: "From the round top of your ship of state, dark and threatening clouds may be seen. Heavy billows, like mountains in the distance, disclose to the leeward huge forms of flinty rocks! That *bolt* drawn, that *chain* broken, and all is lost. *Cling to this day—cling to it*, and to its principles, with the grasp of a storm-tossed mariner to a spar at midnight."

Nowhere in the text does his inclination toward poetry resonate more poignantly than here: "When the dogs in your streets, when the fowls of the air, when the cattle on your hills, when the fish of the sea, and the reptiles that crawl, shall be unable to distinguish the slave from a brute, then will I argue with you that the slave is a man!" One hears in the orator a rhetoric of urgent necessity informed by cadences that seem natural. The passion is bare to the bone.

It was Paul Laurence Dunbar's "Douglass" that first brought me to this man. I came to his work when I was twelve, before Walt Whitman and James Baldwin, a decade or so before engaging the works of Gwendolyn Brooks, Robert Hayden, Elizabeth Bishop, Pablo Neruda, and James Wright. Douglass's voice refracts all the other voices I have deeply embraced through the years, and still his spirit and language reconstitute themselves in my psyche and call up my own need to re-imagine the world and confront it.

DELIVERING THE GOODS | STEWART O'NAN

The novels I go back to over and over are the ones that make me believe fiction can deliver the way life feels—that is, they deliver the whole emotional world of their characters. The depth and precision (and muddle) of *To the Lighthouse*, or the spare clarity of James Salter's *Light Years*. The generosity of William Maxwell toward his people in *So Long, See You Tomorrow*. As daunting as these masterpieces are, tours de force all, they prove to me that it can be done. Just as these same writers' lesser works and failures prove how difficult writing a great novel is.

A MAGNIFICENT NEIGHBOR | ANNE LANDSMAN

In 1979 and 1980, I studied with J.M. Coetzee in the English Department at the University of Cape Town, taking his "Realism in the Novel" class and a seminar on Ezra Pound and T.S. Eliot. I can still see the sun streaking into the classroom, dust motes dancing as we listened to Coetzee's precise voice, the elegant turns and curves of his crystalline intellect. He had a way of carving his questions into the air with devastating simplicity. Quite often, the class was stupefied, perhaps by the heat, perhaps by the difficult times we were living in, perhaps by being nineteen and twenty and not knowing very much about anything.

Or perhaps everyone felt the way I did: heart in my throat, stunned into silence by this small, quiet man's brilliance. His gifts as a writer were becoming known but he had not yet been crowned as one of the greatest writers of our time. When I began to read his novels, I heard his voice speaking the words, the same spare prose he used in the classroom, the same economy and honesty. In this way, he continued to be my teacher and moral compass through the darkest days of apartheid. By that time I was living in the United States, and reading about South Africa—in particular, reading *Life & Times of Michael K*—took me on a journey to the earliest part of myself, to my childhood in Worcester, a small Boland town ringed by mountains. The physical descriptions of the land were searingly familiar, and the excruciating solitude of Michael K so vivid.

In the late '80s, Coetzee gave a reading at Endicott's bookstore on the Upper West Side. I spoke to him there, reminding him I was once a student of his and letting him know I now lived in New York City, writing screenplays. He said drily, "You escaped the UCT English department," and gave a faint smile.

When I began writing my first novel, *The Devil's Chimney*, in 1994, I couldn't help recalling the desiccated landscape of *In the Heart of the Country*, the harsh world of *Waiting for the Barbarians*. But working in his shadow, guided by his influence, was never overwhelming or suffocating.

In 1997, the first of his memoirs, *Boyhood*, was published. I opened to page one, and was electrified by the line, "They live on a housing estate outside the town of Worcester, between the railway line and the National Road." What? J.M. Coetzee lived in Worcester, where I was born and raised? He looked out at the same purple mountains I did, riding his bicycle to school every morning? I could scarcely believe it. I had always felt stretched thin between continents and cultures, and this was a sudden grounding, an affirmation that this town so unknown, so far away from the center of everything, meant something, was a worthy subject. As I read, I ran into familiar landmarks, people I knew, resonant details. The navy blue cap he wore to school with the image of a mountain and stars on it, emblazoned with the legend "Per Aspera Ad Astra," was the same cap my brother wore. Coetzee went to Boswell's Circus too, and the bioscope! Other descriptions were painful and all too familiar—the unabashed racism, the canings of children at school, a father who drank too much.

Over the years, I've continued to read almost everything Coetzee has written, including the speeches he made upon receiving the Nobel Prize. I've delighted in his experimentation with the form of the novel, and reflected on the depth of his moral questioning. But I have never forgotten that shock of recognition, that my town was his town. No wonder I had read *Life & Times of Michael K* as if I was coming home, as if I could see every rock and every crevice up close. No wonder that when I sit down to write, Coetzee is always there, not admonishing, not making suggestions, but silent, a magnificent neighbor.

BOUNDARY ERRORS | SAÏD SAYRAFIEZADEH

I met Ned Frost my freshman year. I was eighteen and had a vague idea that I wanted to be a writer. He hired me to work in the college's administrative office and took, almost instantly, a keen interest in my literary aspirations. He was a large man, bearded and amiable, who thought of himself as an accomplished writer and poet despite never having published—and who hoped, so he confided in me, to soon lead a life in which he could write full-time. To this end he had read all of the classics—Shakespeare, Dante, Montaigne,

Joyce—and he quoted them often and easily when illustrating an idea. In his office, with the door closed, he would lean over his desk and talk to me at length about writing, reading aloud from the masters and from his own work, apparently unconcerned that the job I had been hired to do was being done by other students.

I was taking Writing 101, the prerequisite I had to satisfy before taking the classes that would teach me how to compose plays, novels, essays, memoirs—all of which I was sure I would one day write to great acclaim. The first assignment was a three-page essay on a Wittgenstein axiom: "The limits of my language are the limits of my world." What I wrote was passionate, deeply felt, certainly the best in the class. It was returned the following week with a handwritten note: "There seems to be a problem with sentence boundary errors. If you have trouble with them, I suggest you make an appointment at the writing workshop. See me."

I was infuriated. And humiliated. Back in Ned Frost's office, near tears, I showed him the essay. He read it quickly, hunched over his desk. When he finished he stared down at his hands. Finally he looked up into my eyes and said, "It's beautiful."

After that I showed Ned everything: poems, stories, term papers, journal entries. His praise was abundant and glorious. I was a literary genius, he told me, one of the best writers he had read. I had already surpassed the need for writing courses and teachers and school. They would only try to corral and distract me, he said, with trivial matters like "sentence boundary errors."

In return, he gave me his own writing, which was shockingly bad. Often it took the form of letters—long, convoluted letters, as many as fifteen pages long, that talked about love. Or about loving someone. Possibly loving someone that was me. With no idea what to say, I extolled his writing the same way he extolled mine. One day towards the end of freshman year I received a brief, sexually graphic letter saying that he loved me and that "there is no line I draw between myself and another man."

I was horrified. I threatened to quit. He apologized and promised never to write anything like that again. A few days later he gave me another letter, just as sexually charged. I threatened again. He promised again. So it went. There would be interludes of a week or so in which he ceased his provocations and we returned to the way it had been. But that never lasted. Soon the letters suggested I was gay and didn't realize it. Then they said so overtly. He was convinced. He knew I wanted to sleep with him as much as he wanted to sleep with me. "Boys who grow up without fathers are conflicted about their sexuality," he wrote.

Other students told me I was not the first young, straight man to be pursued by Ned Frost, and that I wouldn't be the last. The more you resisted, the more he chased, they said. On several occasions I left my apartment in the morning to find he had placed a letter in my mailbox during the night. "I saw that your shades were drawn. They are never drawn." I feared I was losing my mind. Sophomore year started and still I couldn't shake him. The truth was I had become dependent on his approval in order to write.

Nearing a nervous breakdown, I finally broke away from him for good. For a while I could not read or write anything without associating it with Ned Frost. I was sure I had been ruined by him, that my ability to write had been permanently damaged and I would never rid his voice from my head.

A year or so later, I ran into a young man on the street who had also once worked for Ned Frost. We shared our stories—which, given the passage of time, now seemed absurd, even comic. He told me he'd been a guitarist and studied music hoping to make a career of it, and that Ned Frost, who considered himself an expert on all the arts, had insinuated himself into his life, praised him endlessly, and tried to convince him he was gay and in love with Ned. "Now I don't ever play guitar," he said.

Standing there on the street, I promised myself I would continue to write, no matter what.

IN THRALL | LILY TUCK

Audrey Hepburn, at the end of *Roman Holiday*, is asked which city is her favorite, and answers, "Rome. By all means, Rome." Asked such a question about writers, my answer is: Joan Didion. By all means, Joan Didion.

I just now reread *A Book of Common Prayer* and once again—the book was published in 1977—was dazzled by the power of understatement and indirection which is so much a trademark of Didion's art.

Withholding, I suppose one calls it.

Who is Charlotte Douglas, the enigmatic woman at the center of the novel? Why did she come to this out-of-the-way Central American country? One never really finds out exactly, and yet, because Didion gives one just enough tantalizing details to guess, to imagine, to make assumptions, the reader is totally in Charlotte's thrall. As are most of the men in the novel.

Here is how Didion describes her:

As a child of comfortable family in the temperate zone, she had been as a matter of course provided with clean sheets, orthodontia, lamb chops, living grandparents, attentive godparents, one brother named Dickie, ballet lessons, and casual timely information about menstruation and the care of flat silver...

No mention is given of her parents, as that would give too much away; parenting, or the lack of it, is, in large part, what the novel is "about," the failure of parents to understand their children. In particular, Charlotte Douglas's failure as a mother is what propels the novel to its tragic end.

I love the quirky, oblique dialogue with the slightly surreal repetitions:

> *We should be doing this all our lives, Warren had said.*
> *We should have done this all our lives, we should do this all our lives.*
> *"I don't want to leave you ever," Charlotte said.*
> *"No," Warren said. "But you will."*
> *After a while there were no more frosts at night and the wild carrot came out along all the roads and every night ended badly.*

In her essay "Why I Write," Didion admits that her attention is always on the periphery, on the specific, the tangible—on what she can see, taste, touch. She writes in order to know what she thinks, she says. I do too.

Joan Didion's writing continues to dazzle and continues to inspire and remind me to look for what is there—then try to leave it out.

WALSER & DARGER | JESSE BALL

One major influence that troubles writers of nearly every era is the pressure to be contemporary. I feel I have two dear friends who help me to live day by day without that trouble, although it is an extreme vanity and affectation to call them friends. Yet, what else are they better suited for? This pair of fine fellows is Robert Walser and Henry Darger. I have but to consider the infinite resources that both have drawn from to be placed again into the frame of mind I long for, wherein making is simply making, and is all the grander for that.

I live in Chicago at this time. Henry Darger is, in my own opinion, by far the best thing about Chicago. You can, if you like, visit a semblance of the room he once lived in, at INTUIT. It is, I must tell you, a powerful experience for those initiated to his life.

If Henry Darger is the master of nesting, then Robert Walser, on the other hand, is the master of tiny handwriting. His microscripts are cunningly marvelous documents that inspire awe, wonder, and jealousy.

I add as well that I don't particularly imagine these two reading my work. That isn't a part of it at all! But their judgments and examples most certainly hang over my life.

ARE YOU MY MOTHER? | ELISSA SCHAPPELL

In P.D. Eastman's *Are You My Mother?* a small brown bird, a latch-key chick who appears to have hatched without the benefit of his parent, goes searching for someone or something on which to imprint. After questioning a cow, an airplane, and a steam shovel, he finally recognizes his mother. Happy ending.

The story isn't unlike my search for a mentor. I had worked with some truly fine professors and had learned much about writing and editing and how to play pool drunk on scotch from George Plimpton at *The Paris Review*. But there was no one I would call a mentor. At times I've wondered if it might not be easier to post an ad in the literary personals. "Wanted: Mentor. Must be devastatingly smart and witty, familiar with city and small-town life. Depressives welcome, no teetotalers, no fundamentalists, no suicides."

If I could find no living writer who epitomized the qualities I aspired to as a writer and a human being I'd search the spirit world. Virginia Woolf had me at wave one. I wanted to write in a style as inventive and poetic as hers, to entwine the personal with the political like she did. I'm not of the same means as Woolf, but like me she was married to a lovely, supportive artistic man, adored her friends and family, and yet, like me, was plagued by depression. She'd walked into the Ouse, though, with her pockets full of stones—successful, well-off, physically fit, and loved. I could attempt, however feebly, to emulate her work, but wouldn't emulate her life.

When I took my first writing job, at *SPY*, the too short-lived satirical monthly, I wished to model myself on Dorothy Parker. Her stingingly witty criticism and essays, her ability to write poetry and fiction that was dark and comic and heartbreaking—her penchant for tossing off bon mots the way an indolent fat lady tosses bonbons, cracking wise even when cracking up, and her radical lefty politics—were all that I aspired to in my early twenties. But her self-loathing and narcissism, her four unsuccessful attempts at suicide, and the fact that her ashes lay unclaimed in the bottom of her lawyer's file cabinet for fifteen years disheartened me.

Ironically my quest for a mentor would end with Dawn Powell, the writer who, according to Diana Trilling, really said "the funny things for which Dorothy Parker gets credit." I didn't discover Powell until 1995. I might never have. Despite her reputation for dissecting the rich better than Fitzgerald, having the satirical gifts of Evelyn Waugh, and being the "best comic writer in America" (according to Gore Vidal), Powell was not especially popular in her lifetime. Her books were mostly out of print when she died. Had a reviewer's copy of *Dawn Powell's Diaries*, edited by Tim Page—who spearheaded the Powell revival—not turned up on my doorstep, I'd have missed her. It was kismet.

Powell was a writer and a woman I could look up to: a brilliant comic writer who wrote about her small hometown as well as her adopted home of New York City. She was a bohemian, a champion cocktailer, devoted mother, steadfast friend. And she was prolific. She wrote fifteen novels, scores of magazine pieces and reviews, ten plays, and more than a hundred stories. Nonetheless, she spent her life on the brink of penury, caring for a severely autistic son, battling chronic health problems and her husband's alcoholism and depression (as well as her own). Yet she wrote. A lot. Beautifully. And never whined.

I confess that I am often frustrated by the notion that it's impossible for a woman to be a wife and mother and first-rate writer. That any female artist who hopes to ever be as highly regarded as her male counterparts should start packing for Bellevue. That any woman who chooses her children's company— nay, relishes it—is a sap who has consigned her Nobel dreams to the scrap heap. It is in these moments I need Dawn Powell the most.

The depression that sent Woolf into the river and sent Parker to an overdose seemed to send Dawn Powell to the typewriter. Not that Powell was any Pollyanna. In her diaries and letters she laments what feels like years wasted on writing that was never appreciated or that failed to meet her high standards. I see the dark fingers of doubt closing around her as often as they do around me. Still, time and again, she rights herself. Within days she is back and writing with the same unswerving intelligence and humor, devoid of anger or pity, just full of hope bolstered by a good day at the typewriter. Onward.

Continued on page 204

Q & A

STRANGE AND DANGEROUS TIMES

Don DeLillo

Don DeLillo received the 2010 PEN/Saul Bellow Award for Achievement in American Fiction. When the award was announced, PEN's Antonio Aiello faxed DeLillo questions about Bellow, his own work, the role of the writer, and more.

ON SAUL BELLOW

I still have my old paperback copy of <u>Herzog</u> (Fawcett Crest, 95¢), a novel I recall reading with great pleasure. It wasn't the first Bellow novel I encountered -- that was <u>The Victim</u>, whose opening sentence ("On some nights New York is as hot as Bangkok.") seemed a novel in itself, at least to a New Yorker. Bellow was a strong force in our literature, making leaps from one book to the next. He was one of the writers who expanded my sense of the American novel's range, or, maybe a better word for Bellow -- its clutch, its grasp -- and it's a special honor to be awarded a prize that bears his name.

ON AMERICAN LANGUAGE

There are many kinds of American fiction and I've always had special admiration for work that attempts to be equal to the sweep of American experience. Sinclair Lewis called for "a literature worthy of

our vastness." A novelist tends to feel this spread
and breadth in his fingertips (or not) and I've
tried to bring a sense of our strange and dangerous
times into my work. I guess I've said before that
I don't think my novels could have been written in
the culture that existed before the assassination
of President Kennedy. I would eventually write about
the event itself and have tried, from the beginning,
to find a language -- an American language -- that
might might carry the ideas and events in my work to
their full potential.

ON TIME AND LOSS

A novel determines its own size and shape and I've
never tried to stretch an idea beyond the frame and
structure it seemed to require. (Underworld wanted
to be big and I didn't attempt to stand in the way.)
The theme that seems to have evolved in my work during
the past decade concerns time -- time and loss. This
was not a plan; the novels have simply tended to edge
in that direction. Some years ago I had the briefest
of exchanges with a professor of philosophy. I
raised the subject of time. He said simply, "Time is
too difficult." Yes, time is a mystery and perhaps
best examined (or experienced by my characters) in
a concise and somewhat enigmatic manner. Next book
may be a monster. (Or just a collection of short
stories.)

ON TECHNOLOGY

The question is whether the enormous force of
technology, and its insistence on speeding up time
and compacting space, will reduce the human need
for narrative -- narrative in the traditional sense.

Novels will become user-generated. An individual
will not only tap a button that gives him a novel
designed to his particular tastes, needs and moods
but he'll also be able to design his own novel,
very possibly with him as main character. The world
is becoming increasingly customized, altered to
individual specifications. This shrinking context
will necessarily change the language that people
speak, write and read. Here's a stray question
(or a metaphysical leap): Will language have the
same depth and richness in electronic form that
it can reach on the printed page? Does the beauty
and variability of our language depend to an important
degree on the medium that carries the words? Does
poetry need paper?

ON RELIGION

The Latin mass had an odd glamour -- all that mystery
and tradition. Religion has not been a major element
in my work, and for some years now I think the true
American religion has been "the American People."
The term quickly developed an aura of sanctity and
inviolability. First used mainly by politicians at
nominating conventions and in inaugural speeches, the
phrase became a mainstay of news broadcasts and other
more or less nonpartisan occasions. All the reverence
once invested in the name of God was transferred to an
entity safely defined as you and me. But do we still
exist? Does the phrase still soar over the airwaves?
Or are the American People dead and buried? It seems
the case, more than ever, that there are only factions,
movements, sects, splinter groups and deeply aggrieved
individual voices. The media absorbs it all.

ON PARANOIA AND DISCONTENT

The earlier era of paranoia in this country was
based largely on violent events and on the suspicions
that spread concerning the true nature of the
particular event, from Dallas to Memphis to Vietnam.
Who was behind it, what led to it, what will flow
from it? How many shots, how many gunmen, how many
wounds on the President's body? People believed,
sometimes justifiably, that they were being lied to
by the government or elements within the government.
Today, it seems, the virus is self-generated. Distrust
and disbelief are centered in a deep need to raise
individual discontent to an art form, often with no
basis in fact. In many cases, people choose to believe
a clear falsehood, about President Obama, for instance,
or September 11, or immigrants, or   Muslims. These
are often symbolic beliefs, usable kinds of fiction,
a means of protest rising from political, economic,
religious or racial complaints, or just a lousy life
in a dying suburb.

ON FREEDOM TO WRITE

The writer's role is to sit in a room and write.
We can leave it at that. Or we can add that writers
have always felt a natural kinship, country to
country, language to language. We can know a country
through its fiction, often a far more telling means
of enlightenment and revelation than any other.
The shelves in the room where I'm writing these
words are crammed with books by foreign writers.
This is work that I've been reading and re-reading
for decades, title after title forming a stream of
warm memories. It's important to remember that we

can also know a country from the writers who are
not permitted to publish their work -- fiction,
nonfiction, journalism -- in accord with honest
observation and clear conscience. Writers who are
subjected to state censorship, threatened with
imprisonment or menaced by violent forces in their
society clearly merit the support of those of us
who enjoy freedom of expression. There are things
a writer never takes for granted, like the long
life he will need to live in order to write the long
novel he is trying to write. Maybe freedom to write
belongs at the top of the list, on behalf of those
writers who face the grim reality of being enemies
of the state.

FICTION

HUMAN MOMENTS
IN WORLD WAR III

Don DeLillo

A note about Vollmer. He no longer describes the earth as a library globe or a map that has come alive, as a cosmic eye staring into deep space. This last was his most ambitious fling at imagery. The war has changed the way he sees the earth. The earth is land and water, the dwelling place of mortal men, in elevated dictionary terms. He doesn't see it anymore (storm-spiraled, sea-bright, breathing heat and haze and color) as an occasion for picturesque language, for easeful play or speculation.

At two hundred and twenty kilometers we see ship wakes and the larger airports. Icebergs, lightning bolts, sand dunes. I point out lava flows and cold-core eddies. That silver ribbon off the Irish coast, I tell him, is an oil slick.

This is my third orbital mission. Vollmer's first. He is an engineering genius, a communications and weapons genius, and maybe other kinds of genius as well. As mission specialist, I'm content to be in charge. (The word *specialist*, in the standard usage of Colorado Command, refers here to someone who does not specialize.) Our spacecraft is designed primarily to gather intelligence. The refinement of the quantum-burn technique enables us to make frequent adjustments of orbit without firing rockets every time. We swing into high wide trajectories, the whole earth as our psychic light, to inspect manned and possibly hostile satellites. We orbit tightly, snugly, take intimate looks at surface activities in untraveled places.

The banning of nuclear weapons has made the world safe for war.

I try not to think big thoughts or submit to rambling abstractions. But the urge sometimes comes over me. Earth orbit puts men into philosophical temper. How can we help it? We see the planet complete. We have a privileged vista. In our attempts to be equal to the experience, we tend to meditate importantly on subjects like the human condition. It makes a man feel *universal*, floating over the continents, seeing the rim of the world, a line as clear as a compass arc, knowing it is just a turning of the bend to Atlantic twilight, to sediment plumes and kelp beds, an island chain glowing in the dusky sea.

I tell myself it is only scenery. I want to think of our life here as ordinary, as a housekeeping arrangement, an unlikely but workable setup caused by a housing shortage or spring floods in the valley.

Vollmer does the systems checklist and goes to his hammock to rest. He is twenty-three years old, a boy with a longish head and close-cropped hair. He talks about northern Minnesota as he removes the objects in his personal-preference kit, placing them on an adjacent Velcro surface for tender inspection. I have a 1901 silver dollar in my personal-preference kit. Little else of note. Vollmer has graduation pictures, bottle caps, small stones from his backyard. I don't know whether he chose these items himself or whether they were pressed on him by parents who feared that his life in space would be lacking in human moments.

Our hammocks are human moments, I suppose, although I don't know whether Colorado Command planned it that way. We eat hot dogs and almond crunch bars and apply lip balm as part of the presleep checklist. We wear slippers at the firing panel. Vollmer's football jersey is a human moment. Outsize, purple and white, of polyester mesh, bearing the number 79, a big man's number, a prime of no particular distinction, it makes him look stoop-shouldered, abnormally long-framed.

"I still get depressed on Sundays," he says.

"Do we have Sundays here?"

"No, but they have them there and I still feel them. I always know when it's Sunday."

"Why do you get depressed?"

"The slowness of Sundays. Something about the glare, the smell of warm grass, the church service, the relatives visiting in nice clothes. The whole day kind of lasts forever."

"I didn't like Sundays either."

"They were slow but not lazy-slow. They were long and hot, or long and cold. In summer my grandmother made lemonade. There was a routine. The whole day was kind of set up beforehand and the routine almost never changed. Orbital routine is different. It's satisfying. It gives our time a shape and substance. Those Sundays were shapeless despite the fact you knew what was coming, who was coming, what we'd all say. You knew the first words out of the mouth of each person before anyone spoke. I was the only kid in the group. People were happy to see me. I used to want to hide."

"What's wrong with lemonade?" I ask.

A battle-management satellite, unmanned, reports high-energy laser activity in orbital sector Dolores. We take out our laser kits and study them for half an hour. The beaming procedure is complex, and because the panel operates on joint control only, we must rehearse the sets of established measures with the utmost care.

A note about the earth. The earth is the preserve of day and night. It contains a sane and balanced variation, a natural waking and sleeping, or so it seems to someone deprived of this tidal effect.

This is why Vollmer's remark about Sundays in Minnesota struck me as interesting. He still feels, or claims he feels, or thinks he feels, that inherently earthbound rhythm.

To men at this remove, it is as though things exist in their particular physical form in order to reveal the hidden simplicity of some powerful mathematical truth. The earth reveals to us the simple awesome beauty of day and night. It is there to contain and incorporate these conceptual events.

Vollmer in his shorts and suction clogs resembles a high school swimmer, all but hairless, an unfinished man not aware he is open to cruel scrutiny, not aware he is without devices, standing with arms folded in a place of echoing voices and chlorine fumes. There is something stupid in the sound of his voice. It is too direct, a deep voice from high in the mouth, slightly insistent, a little loud. Vollmer has never said a stupid thing in my presence. It is just his voice that is stupid, a grave and naked bass, a voice without inflection or breath.

We are not cramped here. The flight deck and crew quarters are thoughtfully designed. Food is fair to good. There are books, videocassettes, news, and music. We do the manual checklists, the oral checklists, the simulated firings with no sign of boredom or carelessness. If anything, we are getting better at our tasks all the time. The only danger is conversation.

I try to keep our conversations on an everyday plane. I make it a point to talk about small things, routine things. This makes sense to me. It seems a sound tactic, under the circumstances, to restrict our talk to familiar topics, minor matters. I want to build a structure of the commonplace. But Vollmer has a tendency to bring up enormous subjects. He wants to talk about war and the weapons of war. He wants to discuss global strategies, global aggressions. I tell him now that he has stopped describing the earth as a cosmic eye he wants to see it as a game board or computer model. He looks at me plain-faced and tries to get me in a theoretical argument: selective space-based attacks versus long, drawn-out, well-modulated land-sea-air engagements. He quotes experts, mentions sources. What am I supposed to say? He will suggest that people are disappointed in the war. The war is dragging into its third week. There is a sense in which it is worn out, played out. He gathers this from the news broadcasts we periodically receive. Something in the announcer's voice hints at a let down, a fatigue, a faint bitterness about—*something*. Vollmer is probably right about this. I've heard it myself in the tone of the broadcaster's voice, in the voice of Colorado Command, despite the fact that our news is censored, that they are not telling us things they feel we shouldn't know, in our special situation, our exposed and sensitive position. In his direct and stupid-sounding and uncannily perceptive way, young Vollmer says that people are not enjoying this war to the same extent that people have always enjoyed and nourished themselves on war, as a heightening, a periodic intensity. What I object to in Vollmer is that he often shares my deep-reaching and most reluctantly held convictions. Coming from that mild face, in that earnest resonant run-on voice, these ideas unnerve and worry me as they never do when they remain unspoken. I want words to be secretive, to cling to a darkness in the deepest interior. Vollmer's candor exposes something painful.

It is not too early in the war to discern nostalgic references to earlier wars. All wars refer back. Ships, planes, entire operations are named after ancient battles, simpler weapons, what we perceive as conflicts of nobler intent. This recon-interceptor is called *Tomahawk II*. When I sit at the firing panel I look at a photograph of Vollmer's granddad when he was a young man in sagging khakis and a shallow helmet, standing in a bare field, a rifle strapped to his shoulder. This is a human moment, and it reminds me that war, among other things, is a form of longing.

We dock with the command station, take on food, exchange cassettes. The war is going well, they tell us, although it isn't likely they know much more than we do.

Then we separate.

The maneuver is flawless and I am feeling happy and satisfied, having resumed human contact with the nearest form of the outside world, having traded quips and manly insults, traded voices, traded news and rumors—buzzers, rumbles, scuttlebutt. We stow our supplies of broccoli and apple cider and fruit cocktail and butterscotch pudding. I feel a homey emotion, putting away the colorfully packaged goods, a sensation of prosperous well-being, the consumer's solid comfort.

Vollmer's t-shirt bears the word INSCRIPTION.

"People had hoped to be caught up in something bigger than themselves," he says. "They thought it would be a shared crisis. They would feel a sense of shared purpose, shared destiny. Like a snowstorm that blankets a large city—but lasting months, lasting years, carrying everyone along, creating fellow feeling where there was only suspicion and fear. Strangers talking to each other, meals by candlelight when the power fails. The war would ennoble everything we say and do. What was impersonal would become personal. What was solitary would be shared. But what happens when the sense of shared crisis begins to dwindle much sooner than anyone expected? We begin to think the feeling lasts longer in snowstorms."

A note about selective noise. Forty-eight hours ago I was monitoring data on the mission console when a voice broke in on my report to Colorado Command. The voice was unenhanced, heavy with static. I checked my headset, checked the switches and lights. Seconds later the command signal resumed and I heard our flight-dynamics officer ask me to switch to the redundant sense frequencer. I did this but it only caused the weak voice to return, a voice that carried with it a strange and unspecifiable poignancy. I seemed somehow to recognize it. I don't mean I knew who was speaking. It was the tone I recognized, the touching quality of some half-remembered and tender event, even through the static, the sonic mist.

In any case, Colorado Command resumed transmission in a matter of seconds.

"We have a deviate, Tomahawk."

"We copy. There's a voice."

"We have gross oscillation here."

"There's some interference. I have gone redundant but I'm not sure it's helping."

"We are clearing an outframe to locate source."

"Thank you, Colorado."

"It is probably just selective noise. You are negative red on the step-function quad."

"It was a voice," I told them.

"We have just received an affirm on selective noise."

"I could hear words in English."

"We copy selective noise."

"Someone was talking, Colorado."

"What do you think selective noise is?"

"I don't know what it is."

"You are getting a spill from one of the unmanneds."

"If it's an unmanned, how could it be sending a voice?"

"It is not a voice as such, Tomahawk. It is selective noise. We have some real firm telemetry on that."

"It sounded like a voice."

"It is supposed to sound like a voice. But it is not a voice as such. It is enhanced."

"It sounded unenhanced. It sounded human in all sorts of ways."

"It is signals and they are spilling from geosynchronous orbit. This is your deviate. You are getting voice codes from twenty-two thousand miles. It is basically a weather report. We will correct, Tomahawk. In the meantime, advise you stay redundant."

About ten hours later Vollmer heard the voice. Then he heard two or three other people in conversation. He gestured to me as he listened, pointed to the headset, then raised his shoulders, held his hands apart to indicate surprise and bafflement. In the swarming noise (as he said later) it wasn't easy to get the drift of what people were saying. The static was frequent, the references were somewhat elusive, but Vollmer mentioned how intensely affecting these voices were, even when the signals were at their weakest. One thing he did know: It wasn't selective noise. A quality of purest, sweetest sadness issued from remote space. He wasn't sure, but he thought there was also a background noise integral to the conversation. Laughter. The sound of people laughing.

In other transmissions we've been able to recognize theme music, an announcer's introduction, wisecracks and bursts of applause, commercials for products whose long-lost brand names evoke the golden antiquity of great cities buried in sand and river silt.

Somehow we are picking up signals from radio programs of forty, fifty, sixty years ago.

Our current task is to collect imagery data on troop deployment. Vollmer surrounds his Hasselblad, engrossed in some microadjustment. There is a seaward bulge of stratocumulus. Sun glint and littoral drift. I see blooms of plankton in a blue of such Persian richness it seems an animal rapture, a color change to express some form of intuitive delight. As the surface features unfurl I list them aloud by name. It is the only game I play in space, reciting the earth names, the nomenclature of contour and structure. Glacial scour, moraine debris. Shatter-coning at the edge of a multi-ring impact site. A resurgent caldera, a mass of castellated rimrock. Over the sand seas now. Parabolic dunes, star dunes, straight dunes with radial crests. The emptier the land, the more luminous and precise the names for its features. Vollmer says the thing science does best is name the features of the world.

He has degrees in science and technology. He was a scholarship winner, an honors student, a research assistant. He ran science projects, read technical papers in the deep-pitched earnest voice that rolls off the roof of his mouth. As mission specialist (generalist), I sometimes resent his nonscientific percep-tions, the glimmering of maturity and balanced judgment. I am beginning to feel slightly preempted. I want him to stick to systems, onboard guidance, data parameters. His human insights make me nervous.

"I'm happy," he says.

These words are delivered with matter-of-fact finality, and the simple statement affects me powerfully. It frightens me, in fact. What does he mean he's happy? Isn't happiness totally outside our frame of reference? How can he think it is possible to be happy here? I want to say to him, "This is just a housekeeping arrangement, a series of more or less routine tasks. Attend to your tasks, do your testing, run through your checklists." I want to say, "Forget the measure of our vision, the sweep of things, the war itself, the terrible death. Forget the overarching night, the stars as static points, as mathematical fields. Forget the cosmic solitude, the upwelling awe and dread."

I want to say, "Happiness is not a fact of this experience, at least not to the extent that one is bold enough to speak of it."

Laser technology contains a core of foreboding and myth. It is a clean sort of lethal package we are dealing with, a well-behaved beam of photons, an engineered coherence, but we approach the weapon with our minds full of ancient warnings and fears. (There ought to be a term for this ironic condition: primitive fear of the weapons we are advanced enough to design and produce.) Maybe this is why the project managers were ordered to work out a firing procedure that depends on the coordinated actions of two men—two tempera-ments, two souls—operating the controls together. Fear of the power of light, the pure stuff of the universe.

A single dark mind in a moment of inspiration might think it liberating to fling a concentrated beam at some lumbering humpbacked Boeing making its commercial rounds at thirty thousand feet.

Vollmer and I approach the firing panel. The panel is designed in such a way that the joint operators must sit back to back. The reason for this, although Colorado Command never specifically said so, is to keep us from seeing each other's face. Colorado wants to be sure that weapons personnel in particular are not influenced by each other's tics and perturbations. We are back to back, therefore, harnessed in our seats, ready to begin, Vollmer in his purple and white jersey, his fleeced pad-abouts.

This is only a test.

I start the playback. At the sound of a prerecorded voice command, we each insert a modal key in its proper slot. Together we count down from five and then turn the keys one-quarter left. This puts the system in what is called an open-minded mode. We count down from three. The enhanced voice says, *You are open-minded now.*

Vollmer speaks into his voiceprint analyzer.

"This is code B for *bluegrass*. Request voice-identity clearance."

We count down from five and then speak into our voiceprint analyzers. We say whatever comes into our heads. The point is simply to produce a voiceprint that matches the print in the memory bank. This ensures that the men at the panel are the same men authorized to be there when the system is in an open-minded mode.

This is what comes into my head: "I am standing at the corner of Fourth and Main, where thousands are dead of unknown causes, their scorched bodies piled in the street."

We count down from three. The enhanced voice says, *You are cleared to proceed to lock-in position.*

We turn our modal keys half right, I activate the logic chip and study the numbers on my screen. Vollmer disengages voiceprint and puts us in voice circuit rapport with the onboard computer's sensing mesh. We count down from five. The enhanced voice says, *You are locked in now.*

As we move from one step to the next a growing satisfaction passes through me—the pleasure of elite and secret skills, a life in which every breath is governed by specific rules, by patterns, codes, controls. I try to keep the results of the operation out of my mind, the whole point of it, the outcome of these sequences of precise and esoteric steps. But often I fail. I let the image in, I think the thought, I even say the word at times. This is confusing, of course. I feel tricked. My pleasure betrayed, as if it had a life of its own, a childlike or intelligent-animal existence independent of the man at the firing panel. We count down from five. Vollmer releases the lever that unwinds the systems-purging disk. My pulse marker shows green at three-second intervals. We count down from three. We turn the modal keys three-quarters right. I activate the beam sequencer. We turn the keys one-quarter right. We count down from three. Bluegrass music plays over the squawk box. The enhanced voice says, *You are moded to fire now.*

We study our world-map kits.

"Don't you sometimes feel a power in you?" Vollmer says. "An extreme state of good health, sort of. An *arrogant* healthiness. That's it. You are feeling so good you begin thinking you're a little superior to other people. A kind of life-strength. An optimism about yourself that you generate almost at the expense of others. Don't you sometimes feel this?"

(Yes, as a matter of fact.)

"There's probably a German word for it. But the point I want to make is that this powerful feeling is so—I don't know—*delicate*. That's it. One day you feel it, the next day you are suddenly puny and doomed. A single little thing goes wrong, you feel doomed, you feel utterly weak and defeated and unable to act powerfully or even sensibly. Everyone else is lucky, you are unlucky, hapless, sad, ineffectual and doomed."

(Yes, yes.)

By chance, we are over the Missouri River now, looking toward the Red Lakes of Minnesota. I watch Vollmer go through his map kit, trying to match the two worlds. This is a deep and mysterious happiness, to confirm the accuracy of a map. He seems immensely satisfied. He keeps saying, "*That's it, that's it.*"

Vollmer talks about childhood. In orbit he has begun to think about his early years for the first time. He is surprised at the power of these memories. As he speaks he keeps his head turned to the window. Minnesota is a human moment. Upper Red Lake, Lower Red Lake. He clearly feels he can see himself there.

"Kids don't take walks," he says. "They don't sunbathe or sit on the porch."

He seems to be saying that children's lives are too well supplied to accommodate the spells of reinforced being that the rest of us depend on. A deft enough thought but not to be pursued. It is time to prepare for a quantum burn.

We listen to the old radio shows. Light flares and spreads across the blue-banded edge, sunrise, sunset, the urban grids in shadow. A man and a woman trade well-timed remarks, light, pointed, bantering. There is a sweetness in the tenor voice of the young man singing, a simple vigor that time and distance and random noise have enveloped in eloquence and yearning. Every sound, every lilt of strings has this veneer of age. Vollmer says he remembers these programs, although of course he has never heard them before. What odd happenstance, what flourish or grace of the laws of physics enables us to pick up these signals? Traveled voices, chambered and dense. At times they have the detached and surreal quality of aural hallucination, voices in attic rooms, the complaints of dead relatives. But the sound effects are full of urgency and verve. Cars turn dangerous corners, crisp gunfire fills the night. It was, it is, wartime. Wartime for Duz and Grape-Nuts Flakes. Comedians make fun of the way the enemy talks. We hear hysterical mock German, moonshine Japanese. The cities are in light, the listening millions fed, met comfortably in drowsy rooms, at war, as the night comes softly down. Vollmer says he recalls specific moments, the comic inflections, the announcer's fat-man laughter. He recalls individual voices rising from the laughter of the studio audience, the cackle of a St. Louis businessman, the brassy wail of a high-shouldered blonde just arrived in California, where women wear their hair this year in aromatic bales.

Vollmer drifts across the wardroom upside down, eating an almond crunch.

He sometimes floats free of his hammock, sleeping in a fetal crouch, bumping into walls, adhering to a corner of the ceiling grid.

"Give me a minute to think of the name," he says in his sleep.

He says he dreams of vertical spaces from which he looks, as a boy, at— *something.* My dreams are the heavy kind, the kind that are hard to wake from, to rise out of. They are strong enough to pull me back down, dense enough to leave me with a heavy head, a drugged and bloated feeling. There are episodes of faceless gratification, vaguely disturbing.

It's almost unbelievable when you think of it, how they live there in all that ice and sand and mountainous wilderness. "Look at it," he says. "Huge barren deserts, huge oceans. How do they endure all those terrible things? The floods alone. The earthquakes alone make it crazy to live there. Look at those fault systems. They're so big, there's so many of them. The volcanic eruptions alone. What could be more frightening than a volcanic eruption? How do they endure avalanches, year after year, with numbing regularity? It's hard to believe people live there. The floods alone. You can see whole huge discolored areas, all flooded out, washed out. How do they survive, where do they go? Look at the cloud buildups. Look at that swirling storm center. What about the people who live in the path of a storm like that? It must be packing incredible winds. The lightning alone. People exposed on beaches, near trees and telephone poles. Look at the cities with their spangled lights spreading in all directions. Try to imagine the crime and violence. Look at the smoke pall hanging low. What does that mean in terms of respiratory disorders? It's crazy. Who would live there? The deserts, how they encroach. Every year they claim more and more arable land. How enormous those snowfields are. Look at the massive storm fronts over the ocean. There are ships down there, small craft, some of them. Try to imagine the waves, the rocking. The hurricanes alone. The tidal waves. Look at those coastal communities exposed to tidal waves. What could be more frightening than a tidal wave? But they live there, they stay there. Where could they go?"

I want to talk to him about calorie intake, the effectiveness of the earplugs and nasal decongestants. The earplugs are human moments. The apple cider and the broccoli are human moments. Vollmer himself is a human moment, never more so than when he forgets there is a war.

The close-cropped hair and longish head. The mild blue eyes that bulge slightly. The protuberant eyes of long-bodied people with stooped shoulders. The long hands and wrists. The mild face. The easy face of a handyman in a panel truck that has an extension ladder fixed to the roof and a scuffed license plate, green and white, with the state motto beneath the digits. That kind of face.

He offers to give me a haircut. What an interesting thing a haircut is, when you think of it. Before the war there were time slots reserved for such activities. Houston not only had everything scheduled well in advance but constantly monitored us for whatever meager feedback might result. We were wired, taped, scanned, diagnosed, and metered. We were men in space, objects worthy of the most scrupulous care, the deepest sentiments and anxieties.

Now there is war. Nobody cares about my hair, what I eat, how I feel about the spacecraft's décor, and it is not Houston but Colorado we are in touch with. We are no longer delicate biological specimens adrift in an alien environment. The enemy can kill us with its photons, its mesons, its charged particles faster than any calcium deficiency or trouble of the inner ear, faster than any dusting of micrometeoroids. The emotions have changed. We've stopped being candidates for an embarrassing demise, the kind of mistake or unforeseen event that tends to make a nation grope for the appropriate response. As men in war, we can be certain, dying, that we will arouse uncomplicated sorrows, the open and dependable feelings that grateful nations count on to embellish the simplest ceremony. A note about the universe. Vollmer is on the verge of deciding that our planet is alone in harboring intelligent life. We are an accident and we happened only once. (What a remark to make, in egg-shaped orbit, to someone who doesn't want to discuss larger questions.) He feels this way because of the war.

The war, he says, will bring about an end to the idea that the universe swarms, as they say, with life. Other astronauts have looked past the star points and imagined infinite possibility, grape-clustered worlds teeming with higher forms. But this was before the war. Our view is changing even now, his and mine, he says, as we drift across the firmament.

Is Vollmer saying that cosmic optimism is a luxury reserved for periods between world wars? Do we project our current failure and despair out toward the star clouds, the endless night? After all, he says, where are they? If they exist, why has there been no sign, not one, not any, not a single indicator that serious people might cling to, not a whisper, a radio pulse, a shadow? The war tells us it is foolish to believe.

Our dialogues with Colorado Command are beginning to sound like computer-generated teatime chat. Vollmer tolerates Colorado's jargon only to a point. He is critical of their more debased locutions and doesn't mind letting them know. Why, then, if I agree with his views on this matter, am I becoming irritated by his complaints? Is he too young to champion the language? Does he have the experience, the professional standing to scold our flight-dynamics officer, our conceptual-paradigm officer, our status consultants on waste-management systems and evasion-related zonal options? Or is it something else completely, something unrelated to Colorado Command and our communications with them? Is it the sound of his voice? Is it just his *voice* that is driving me crazy?

Vollmer has entered a strange phase. He spends all his time at the window now, looking down at the earth. He says little or nothing. He simply wants to look, do nothing but look. The oceans, the continents, the archipelagos. We are configured in what is called a cross-orbit series and there is no repetition from one swing around the earth to the next. He sits there looking. He takes meals at the window, barely glancing at the instruction sheets as we pass over tropical storms, over grass fires and major ranges. I keep waiting for him to return to his prewar habit of using quaint phrases to describe the earth: it's a beach ball, a sun-ripened fruit. But he simply looks out the window, eating almond crunches, the wrappers floating away. The view clearly fills his consciousness. It is powerful enough to silence him, to still the voice that rolls off the roof of his mouth, to leave him turned in the seat, twisted uncomfortably for hours at a time.

The view is endlessly fulfilling. It is like the answer to a lifetime of questions and vague cravings. It satisfies every childlike curiosity, every muted desire, whatever there is in him of the scientist, the poet, the primitive seer, the watcher of fire and shooting stars, whatever obsessions eat at the night side of his mind, whatever sweet and dreamy yearning he has ever felt for nameless places far away, whatever earth sense he possesses, the neural pulse of some wilder awareness, a sympathy for beasts, whatever belief in an immanent vital force, the Lord of Creation, whatever secret harboring of the idea of human oneness, whatever wishfulness and simple-hearted hope, whatever of too much and not enough, all at once, and little by little, whatever burning urge to escape responsibility and routine, escape his own overspecialization, the circumscribed and inward-spiraling self, whatever remnants of his boyish longing to fly, his dreams of strange spaces and eerie heights, his fantasies of happy death, whatever indolent and sybaritic leanings, lotus-eater, smoker of grasses and herbs, blue-eyed gazer into space—all these are satisfied, all collected and massed in that living body; the sight he sees from the window.

"It is just so interesting," he says at last. "The colors and all."

The colors and all.

CONVERSATION

RIMBAUD'S CALLING CARD

JONATHAN LETHEM: Patti, I want to start by making you talk about being a book scout. One of my favorite things in your memoir *Just Kids* was not just the fact that you were scuffling for rare books to make money, but your descriptions of those books: You say the pages were lightly foxed, or all the plates were in place. It made me remember my own days as a book hound, imagining what I could turn over some item for.

PATTI SMITH: Well, I grew up in the '50s, when most people in America were getting rid of their old stuff. They didn't want their grandfather's or their parents' stuff. They didn't want the nice porcelain; they wanted Melmac. They didn't want these old leather-bound books; they wanted the *Reader's Digest* collection. So even as a child I would go to rummage sales or church bazaars and pick out books for pennies, for a quarter. I got a first edition Dickens with a green velvet cover and a tissue guard with a gravure of Dickens. You could get things like that. It has never gone away, my love of the book. The paper, the font, the cloth covers. All of these things are slowly dying out.

LETHEM: And did you work at rare book shops at one point?

SMITH: I only worked at one: Argosy Book Store, in 1967. Though I falsified my credentials as a book restorer. The old fellow who ran Argosy was very touched by me and he tried to train me, but I spilled rabbit glue all over a nineteenth-century Bible. He said it was not really rare, though; it was just a trainer Bible. Still, he had to let me go.

LETHEM: And you still collect precious artifacts? You showed me a few amazing things earlier. Patti let me hold Arthur Rimbaud's calling card this morning.

SMITH: I have such nice things. I have a couple of letters of H.P. Lovecraft's,

This transcript was adapted from a conversation that took place at the 2010 PEN World Voices Festival.

a watercolor of Hermann Hesse's, a page from Jim Morrison's last notebook. All of these things we don't really own; we have a guardianship of them for a while. I look at them, I play with them.

LETHEM: I always feel that the collector's role connects very strongly to something curatorial. You've been a collage artist your whole life: You've cut things up to make other things out of them, you've been an appropriator. In gestures as simple as recording "Hey Joe" and "Gloria" among your first songs—as a cover artist, you're a remixer. And to collect things is also to want to repurpose them.

SMITH: I know of people who own rare manuscripts and keep them in vaults. All my stuff is in my room. I look at my things, love them, let them live outside of a metal box. Sometimes I photograph them. That's my way of appropriating things like that. I did naughtily appropriate a nineteenth-century mathematics book of the Riemann Hypothesis for a collage, but it was falling apart anyway.

LETHEM: I've just read your gorgeous account of the origins of your collaborative work—and collaborative life, really—with Robert Mapplethorpe. You're known now as a musician and a writer, but you still take photographs. Do you still draw as well?

SMITH: Oh, yes. It's funny because I don't consider myself a musician at all. I can play a few chords on the guitar. I have no natural gifts as a musician. Obviously I sing, but I think of myself more as a performer. In terms of my real skills, I would think of myself as a writer and a visual artist before I would a musician.

LETHEM: Were you ever an art student in any capacity?

SMITH: I studied art history at Glassboro State Teachers College. And then I came to New York in 1967, and really I studied through Robert. I was drawing at the time. We sat for hours and hours, night after night, drawing. And I studied in my own way. One of my ideas when I came to New York in 1967 was to get a job at the Museum of Modern Art as a guide. I knew the story and history of every painting in the Museum of Modern Art, and I tried to pitch that as a job, but they scooted me out. I, like you, was an unruly student, but I always dreamed of going to Pratt. I couldn't afford to. I couldn't get a scholarship, as I wasn't the best of students.

LETHEM: This is a generic question to ask, but I'd be interested in knowing what your writing process is like, how you put the book together, and whether you are working on another book like it, or want to write another book in the same mode.

SMITH: This book was very difficult because Robert asked me to write it. He asked me to write it on his deathbed. I wanted to write it. I have lots of sources, I have daily diaries. I know the date when I cut his hair, when I first chopped off my hair, when I first met Janis Joplin, when Robert went to a taxi dance. I have lengthy journals, I have his letters. But after Robert died I had to face the death of my husband, my brother, and my parents. And I found it very difficult to write. It's only been in the last few years when all these notes and pages and baskets of writings—I was able to sit and put them all together. And I made two rules for myself: One, that no matter what I remember or what I had, that if I couldn't see what I was writing about as a little movie then I took it away. Because I wanted the reader to enter the book like they were reading a movie. And the second: Robert was not much of a reader, he didn't read hardly at all, so it couldn't be boring or too digressional or he would just be agitated. He'd say, "Patti…" For instance, I had a two-page meditation on Nathaniel Hawthorne's desk in there, don't ask me why, but I knew it had to go. I can put it somewhere else, but I knew it would just stop the reader—and also agitate Robert.

LETHEM: I was talking about your art as collage, and in a sense this was a collaboration with your own past self. You were collaging these journals and notebooks and letters.

SMITH: And the book is filtered through our relationship. You asked me would I write another. And I didn't think I'd write another, but I couldn't stop writing once I'd become friendly with my voice in the book. I'm still writing, but what I decided to do is to write maybe a little trilogy of books that all are in the same time period, but from a different angle. I could write about that whole time period again, but not filtered through Robert and me—it would engage with other things: how I wrote songs, or other things that happened.

LETHEM: There are others who seem to become pivotal who you just allude to, like Sam Shepard.

SMITH: Right. Or I could write a whole chapter on William Burroughs. Both you and I love Bolaño's *2666*. It's such a freeing book for a writer. It suggests the idea of entering and reentering and exiting worlds. I thought it'd be interesting to expand the world that I began. If people want it. And it seems like they might. I like your sneakers.

LETHEM: Thank you. They're not vintage.

SMITH: Doesn't matter, they're classic.

LETHEM: That's the word. Speaking of my Ramones sneakers—I was ten years old in 1974. I went to CBGB's three or four years later for the first time.

SMITH: You went to CBGB's when you were thirteen? I'm sorry!

LETHEM: Oh, it's OK.

SMITH: I wasn't even let out of the house when I was thirteen.

LETHEM: Well it was only a subway ride. But the way that my friends and I received your career, which was already legendary to us in '76, '77, is that you had graduated—you and the Talking Heads would not appear in a small club anymore. We'd have to go to Winterland or some place.

SMITH: That's not true, I still went back right to the end. It's just that I was often on the road, that's all. It wasn't a philosophy.

LETHEM: We were more often in those little clubs seeing our own peers, high school students who had started bands were now taking over CBGB's. And we would see you guys in these little mini-arenas. But the concept of punk was so formative for us. It was so powerful. It created a possibility for us as listeners, and as a subculture—we could claim our own rock and roll. And that also had an adolescent-quarantine aspect to it. Certain things were decisively "uncool" or unacceptable. We didn't let ourselves hear how great the music that preceded punk was. We needed it to be our own anthemic thing. Of course, reading your story it's amazing to see—it shouldn't be shocking, but it was because of the prejudices I find I still have from that punk identity—how completely continuous you see it with the earlier rock and roll: '50s and '60s, and even early '70s, Janis Joplin being a great example. The development of your role as a performer, as the singer in a rock and roll band, didn't come from sweeping the plate clean.

SMITH: I love hearing about this, because people like Lenny Kaye and myself, we were born in 1946. We saw, from childhood on, the entire evolution of rock and roll. So when we started performing in '73 and '74, we were not punk rock. We were guardians, we felt, of our own history. We felt that rock and roll was becoming more corporate, more glamorous, less a cultural voice. We wanted to remind people that it was a grassroots art. That it was ours, that it was revolutionary, that it belonged to the people. It didn't belong to rich rock stars, it didn't belong to the record companies, it belonged to the people. Please don't get me wrong, I'm not comparing us to Moses, but Lenny and I often thought that we saw the promised land, we saw the future for generations. We saw rock and roll as belonging to the streets. Just people playing in their garages. Anyone could play rock and roll.

We were more the bridge. The people that came after, like the Sex Pistols: I knew all those kids, they came to our shows. I knew the Clash. But for a lot of them, it was necessary, as you said, to turn their back on their past because of their method. They had to break through without us, and even despise us. And I understood that. But I'm not like that. To me, being part of the chain that includes anyone from Raphael, to Coltrane, to Allen Ginsberg, to Jimi Hendrix—to be part of this is something that I embrace. I wouldn't want to turn all of that over. But I have no quarrel with people who need to do that. It's up to the individual and how one declares her existence. Sometimes one has to disengage in order to declare. I did that with religion just like certain new groups did to my band or to the so-called dinosaurs of rock and roll. But it's all OK, as long as we keep the blood infused in the medium.

LETHEM: For a teenage listener you were on the side of revolution at that time. We would have placed your relationship to the dinosaurs of rock and roll as a very aggressive one. And the irony is that you have always been so engaged with your sources, whether it's William Blake or Van Morrison, you've always worn them on your sleeve and celebrated them in a sort of ecstatic way. By combining them with an image of renewal and revolution you can also become a guide back to those sources for someone. What is your relationship to present-day music making? Do you listen to a lot of contemporary music when you think about what kind of recording you might make?

SMITH: No. I listen to opera, really. That's what I listen to. And I listen to my son and daughter. My daughter is twenty-two years old, and she's composing all the time. I listen to her playing, I listen to her friends. My son is a guitar player. They stick stuff on my computer. I'm listening to my opera and then one day there's the Yeah Yeah Yeahs. So, OK, I'll listen to that. The other thing I do is I have a MySpace page, and I'm not so active on it, but I have all these friends on MySpace, and a lot of them create their own music and I listen to them, I see what they're doing. I tour; a lot of young kids give me their CDs. People ask me, "Who are the new people?" To me, the new people are the unknown people. The new people that I embrace are the people that we don't even know—the people of the future, the kids who are in their basements, or the group that's struggling out there in Brooklyn. It's an abstract thing, but they're the people I invest my love in.

LETHEM: You just mentioned your kids. One of the things I find so stirring, having grown up with your career as a fan, is that there is a mysterious period in the middle where you became primarily the member of a family.

SMITH: A housewife.

LETHEM: A suburban housewife.

SMITH: Wasn't quite suburban.

LETHEM: I thought I'd try. So there's *Dream of Life* as this weird signal coming out of that in the middle, this incredible album—and as we now know you suffered losses and transformations, but you also came back to a time of fertile productivity. And you have this relationship to your grown children, who play music on stage with you at times. This is great for people who have an alienated romance that to be creative is to be outside of a family, to not have children—it's something only young people do and you have to make a choice. Well, the story of your choices is a stirring one—but it's also incomplete. We don't know how you felt about moving out of New York and out of the role that you carved for yourself in the career that you had here.

SMITH: Well, the role that I carved for myself we had accomplished. In terms of rock and roll, our mission was to wake people up and make new space for the new guard. The new guard came and hopefully we created space for them. So I felt that I had accomplished that mission. And being on the road and starting to become quite successful—the demands and pressure of that, and the media—I felt that I wasn't growing as an artist at all. I wasn't growing politically, I wasn't growing spiritually. And I met a great person, Fred "Sonic" Smith. He had been in the MC5, he had gone through all of the things that I had gone through. And I had a decision: Did I want to carve a more difficult life with this man, or continue the way I was going? And I most happily went with him.

I missed New York City. I love New York City. I missed the coffee shops,

I missed the camaraderie with my band. But it's a misconception that those were not productive years. This book *Just Kids* came from those sixteen years of developing a writer's discipline, of becoming, I hope, a better human being, of having children and finding I wasn't the center of the universe, being more empathetic to my fellow man. I became more knowledgeable politically, just seeing how human beings toil. I had to do all the cooking and the cleaning and the washing of the diapers. We didn't have nannies or anything like that; we did everything ourselves. We didn't make a big income because we both withdrew from public life. But for me, the skills and disciplines that I obtained in those years have magnified all of my efforts. So they certainly weren't lost years.

LETHEM: That's a beautiful way to put it. I want to talk a little bit about your reading life. You're so engaged with Roberto Bolaño right now, and you've talked about how you tend to have this consuming relationship with very, very large books in succession. You spent, you described it as a year, reading over and over again Hermann Hesse's *The Glass Bead Game*. And now that it's Bolaño, you can't get away from *2666*. But I also have heard that you reread certain children's books over and over again.

SMITH: Oh, yes, all the time. I walk with all my books. I reread. I love *A Child's Garden of Verses*, I love *Songs of Innocence*. Which isn't a children's book, but my mother gave it to me as a child so I perceived it as a children's book. *Pinocchio*, *Alice in Wonderland*, *Peter Pan*. My goal in life, still, which I haven't achieved, and I've wanted this ever since I was ten, is to write one of those books. I really hope I live long enough to give to the children of the future one wonderful book that they'll love as much as I love *Pinocchio*. I've always loved books. *Moby-Dick* I guess was the first big book that I plowed through—rereading "The Whiteness of the Whale," skipping the whaling chapters.

LETHEM: The blubber.

SMITH: There's nothing more wonderful to me than that book.

LETHEM: You mentioned William Blake. You wrote a song about him?

SMITH: I wrote this little song when I felt unappreciated. Which I know might seem ridiculous because obviously I'm well appreciated—but it's all relative, you know, sometimes you feel unappreciated. And I was feeling sorry for myself. I fell asleep and when I woke up this song was in my head—and it was the answer. The answer was? Remember William Blake, who gave us such beautiful songs, poems; who was an activist, a humanist, a philosopher, an artist, a printer—and also a casualty of the Industrial Revolution; and who barely had any success in his own lifetime, was ridiculed, died penniless, and was nearly forgotten. And yet William Blake was always grateful for his visionary powers, never let them go, and did his work even on his deathbed. He was working on illustrations to Dante, still speaking to his angels. So I try to remember William Blake when I feel sorry for myself, which isn't too often.

LETHEM: I've been hogging you. Any questions?

AUDIENCE: Could you talk about the connection between Allen Ginsberg, William Blake, and Walt Whitman—that lineage and your part in that?

SMITH: Actually, Allen, who was my great friend and teacher, used to talk about this. We have two trees: We have the genetic, family tree and we have the spiritual, artist, golden-chain tree. It's like you can choose your ancestors. Allen really felt this connection. We used to play a game: Who are your ancestors? His were, of course, Walt Whitman and William Blake. And each of them—William Blake, Walt Whitman, and Allen Ginsberg—all three of these men reached out to all of us, past, present, and future, to animate our creative impulse. Walt Whitman called to future young poets yet to be born, "I am with you now." Allen Ginsberg embraced that. And he walked with Walt Whitman, with William Blake. I think of them all. I did a lot of walking with William Burroughs.

AUDIENCE: Patti, I am from the former Soviet Union, so first I want to tell you what a big role you and Robert Mapplethorpe and your generation played for us when we were starting our own revolution in the '80s and '90s. We fought the Soviets because we knew about you guys in the '60s and '70s. It was the same spirit of liberation from this slavery. You guys—Janis Joplin, all those guys—were for us; not Ronald Reagan and Maggie Thatcher, that's bullshit. It was you guys who generated this revolution in the Soviet Union. My question is simple: In 2010, are we condemned to live in bourgeois slavery?

SMITH: I don't think we're condemned to do anything. As long as we're alive we have choices. Actually, I don't even know what bourgeois slavery is since I've never experienced it, so I'm not quite sure exactly what that means. But I think each generation has to translate for themselves. I myself never felt condemned to anything. I always felt like no matter the situation, one could imagine or create her own portal out of there. We have either our own physical ability to change, or we have our imagination in times of imprisonment. That's the only thing I can say about that.

AUDIENCE: How do you experience limitations to freedom of expression? You are a wonderful free spirit, and you write wonderful words, but there are so many restrictions to freedom of speech, either visible and institutionalized, or invisible and informal.

SMITH: I don't know, I'm lucky. Being an American I have obviously enjoyed freedom of speech as part of our heritage. Of course, one has to continuously fight for this. And people did die in the revolution in this country. But sometimes people ask me that and all they're talking about is a record company doesn't want them to put a certain song on their CD. Well, fuck 'em. Put it on or leave. You just keep doing your work. If a corporation or a big company won't put out your work, you go out in the streets. Before I had a record label we made our own records and went to parks and sold them for a dollar, or read poems out in the streets, and I still do that. I still go all over the world and will go to a square with my guitar and just sing a song. We are a lot less confined than people think. Obviously there are some cultures where that's not true. But here we are a lot less confined. You just have to keep pushing—as Jim Morrison said, "Break on through to the other side."

AUDIENCE: I want to thank you for writing about your experience when you were nineteen. I'm nineteen as well and also lost a child over the past year, and I appreciate how your strength prevailed, how your creative expression didn't die down—you didn't let your depression get in the way after a traumatic experience like giving up a child for adoption. I admire your strength and your ability to share that.

SMITH: It was a hard choice to talk about it, but it's nothing I'm ashamed of. It was very painful, and I also wanted to protect all of the people involved. The things that happen to us when we're young do seem exquisitely painful, and sometimes we feel we won't get over it. I cried, really, for two years. Didn't even know why I was crying. But we prevail. Human beings are so strong; the things that we have gone through in the evolution of becoming human beings. And believe me, in your life you will suffer again—but you will have a million wonderful things happen. A lot of rough things have happened in my life, but I don't look at them as the stepping stones of becoming a human being. You just try to pick the beautiful things. You're given life: your first sense of your own imagination, your first sense of God, your first feeling of love. Even the beauty of feeling when you lose somebody, you feel them in your heart. Pain is an important part of being human; you wouldn't want to live without it. It's why the seasons are beautiful.

AUDIENCE: Can you talk about your experience of finding a discipline as an artist and a writer? I think it's a generally gruesome and painful and awful experience.

SMITH: You mean the discipline of work?

AUDIENCE: Yeah, finding a routine.

SMITH: I worked steady jobs since I was fourteen, from '62 to '73, so I've experienced the nine-to-five job. That was the real painful experience of discipline. The mind and the heart and the imagination are all muscles and they must be exercised. And I think it's important to set goals for ourselves. I made a vow with myself when I was very young that I had to write something every day, even if it was a piece of conversation from others—even if I had nothing to say myself, to be attentive to what people were saying, or to record a dream when I woke up in the morning. And I can honestly say that for about 90 percent of my life I've written at least one line. Sometimes several pages, sometimes literally four words. It's the happy prison of existence. Sometimes I pretend I'm a prisoner and if I don't write my word I'm going to get solitary confinement. In any event, whatever game you play with yourself, discipline is a beautiful thing. It's like people who do a lot of yoga or exercising, after a while your body craves that. And if you sit and make yourself look at a blank page, or write, or look at your canvas, or your violin, and work with it just a little, after a time you'll crave it. And buy yourself a nice pen and notebook.

FICTION

THE DISAPPEARING BRIDE AND OTHER STORIES

Helen Phillips

1

Today being married to you makes my heart feel like a cucumber, long and cold and awkwardly shaped for the cavity in which it belongs. The new brides are not interested in my advice. They tell me to buzz off. Their nails are encrusted with diamonds that will be thrown away at the end of the day. If I knew where they'd be washing their hands, I'd follow them and gather those diamonds. They're tiny, and yellowish in color, but nonetheless.

Because I am so difficult, we go to a motel. In the motel, there you feel free. Yet I and my cucumber fail you again. We leave at 5:17 AM after a few hours of terrifying sleep, during which your limbs strewn over me feel like a hot, fleshy web. (In the past, your arms and legs always served as a shield of blood and bone, defending me from nightmares.) I gasp, my eyes so dry they feel like knives.

The streets are murky. You could have picked a different bride. Yet here we are, burdened with luggage, limping, and I am insisting that I need a notebook, a pencil, a table, in order to record phrases such as: "Today being married to you makes my heart feel like X."

At sunup, we find ourselves alongside a wide black river where a boat bearing a bridal party moves eastward, gleaming. You take me to an old library with a heavy wooden desk. The ghost of our future daughter runs naughtily down the stone hallway. You chase her, feeding her bits of banana. I try to write: "during which your limbs strewn over me felt like X X, X X." But I cannot recall! "My X so X they felt like X." I'd had something to say about the sound of many doors slamming. I'd wanted to attack you with sharp questions. I'd wanted to know precisely why you hadn't selected one of the other, better brides. Our nonexistent daughter! She's so noisy, playing hide-and-go-seek with you.

2

A cupcake and a bottle of scotch stood on a subway platform. In the fluorescence, the scotch lacked its rich amber glow. It looked orange and muted, teetering dangerously on the platform's edge. The cupcake pushed the bottle of scotch back to safety, smudging its lavender frosting in the process. To everyone else, the bottle of scotch looked like a drunk young man with bloodshot eyes and a wrinkled shirt; the cupcake looked like a tired young woman with bloodshot eyes and a tense neck. But the bottle of scotch and the cupcake knew they were a bottle of scotch and cupcake. Embarrassed, the cupcake inched away from the bottle of scotch and stared wistfully at a normal couple. "A cupcake and a bottle of scotch stood on a subway platform. That sounds like the beginning of a bad joke," the cupcake said. "Or a great joke," slurred her companion. "Don't fall, idiot!" the cupcake muttered. "Love me!" the bottle of scotch implored.

A man in a suit and a naked woman stood on a subway platform. In the fluorescence, her limbs looked thick and awkward, but under milder light, she'd be lovely. They embraced. "Goodbye." "Goodbye." "I'll never see you again, will I?" To everyone else, the man in the suit looked like a man in a suit and the naked woman looked like a woman in a dress. But the man in the suit and the naked woman knew he wore a suit while she wore nothing. "Are you cold?" Down the tunnel, the train's howling white eyes appeared.

Long after midnight, I am awoken by the sound of your shivering body. Yes, it makes an actual sound. I can hear the racket of your bones. Why didn't you get under the covers, idiot? Your body is too drunk to realize how cold it is, so I must realize it. Come here, idiot, get in, crawl in, I'll hold you until your blood turns from scotch back into blood, until your bones turn from icicles back into bones.

3

Once there was a person whose sadness was so enormous she knew it would kill her if she didn't squeeze it into a cube one centimeter by one centimeter by one centimeter. Diligently, she set about this task. Alone in her room, she grappled with her sadness. It was quite a beast, alternately foggy and slippery; by the time she managed to grip it, her skin was sleek with sweat, soaked with tears. (The sounds coming from her apartment worried the neighbors. *What was that shy little woman up to?*) She twisted her sadness like a dishrag. It strained against her, tugged, pulled. She sat on her sadness to shrink it down the way old-fashioned ladies sat on their snakeskin suitcases.

Then, finally, there it was: a small white cube.

She slipped it into her pocket, went outside, noticed orange lichen growing on tenements, ordered lemonade in a café. The black-and-white checkered floors nearly blinded her—they looked exactly like joy, and she almost covered her eyes. But instead, she fingered the thing in her pocket. Her eyes became bright prisms; they made her irresistible, and soon she had a friend. One day, passing some kids in the street who had just lost a die down the sewer, she discovered a die in her pocket. "Wow, lady," they said. "Where'dya get a blank die?"

"Gosh," she said, "I really can't remember." And she couldn't.

You know that book where they went all over the world and took pictures of families in front of their homes along with everything they owned? A hut in Kenya, a suburban house in Texas, a Tokyo apartment? I always loved to see the precious and unprecious items, the woven blankets and the TVs, the families standing nervously alongside. Sometimes I look around our home and imagine everything out on the street. But I hope that someday, when they come to take our picture with everything we own, it will just be us, standing before a building, your arm around me, a blank die in my palm.

4

He slams her face into a maple tree until the bark is imprinted in her skin. She becomes a maple tree. He taps her for syrup. She poisons her sap. He falls beside a stream. She becomes the stream. He vomits in the stream. She slaps his face. He feels rejuvenated by the water and goes to punish the tree. She becomes a honeybee and stings him. He yanks her wings off.

She robs a bank and brings the money home. He buys champagne and calls the police. She escapes from prison, finds a glass bottle, and searches for him. He gets a job as a clown. She can't smash him with the bottle while he's surrounded by children. He juggles swords and glares at her. She goes home and crawls into bed.

He sits on her and sings songs with hateful lyrics. She pours boiling water over his sleeping body. He becomes a poisonous teabag in her teacup. She drinks tea and falls into a dead sleep. He drags her to the bathtub and drops the hairdryer in. She gets electrocuted and becomes a terrible fire. He flees the bathroom. She devours the towels, then pursues him. He becomes a drip on the leaky ceiling. She approaches, radiant flames howling up the walls. He evaporates. She explodes out the front door. He becomes a rainstorm.

She races down the block, burning desperately. He mists. She rages through intersections, searching. He drizzles. She sees some litter and, suspecting it's him, burns it. He rains and rains. She realizes the rain is him. He pours down. She leaps up. He smokes and steams. She sputters and gasps.

Two marble statues appear in someone's yard. A man and a woman. They're splendid. A miracle of the Lord. Many poor, sad people come to place marigolds and copper coins at their feet. The marble man and woman gaze at each other with a look that cannot be mistaken. That look—it helps people. Their hearts become strong, and marigolds pile up in the yard.

5

In this version of the story, the bride wishes to disappear into the faux groves at the plant nursery. Someone has had the idea of placing two slender white-barked trees on either side of the altar so it will look as though the ceremony is taking place in a delicate forest. Perhaps it was her idea. But now, hearing the others discuss it with the plant nursery employee, she finds it offensively stupid. The bride walks away, toward the trees with their roots aboveground and wrapped in white plastic; white fabric will swathe her head twenty-four hours from now. She strolls among the rows. Her heart cries out like a drowning fish. She hears them yelling in the distance, but chooses to attribute the mournful repetitions of her name to the trees themselves.

The rows end at the beach. She steps out onto gray sand where gray waves hit again and again. A chubby mermaid sits on the beach, her tail as pungent as fish skin in a trashcan. Her hair is the color of pennies and she uses a rock to draw cryptic symbols in the sand, diamonds inside circles… Getting weak coffee in a fishy little seaside café this morning with her parents and future in-laws, everyone talking, making plans, the bride noticed on the wall above them a bad painting of a mermaid drawing cryptic symbols in the sand, the mermaid's arms thick and awkward… The bride discovers that the mermaid has vanished from the beach, along with the cryptic symbols. Her heart cries out like a drowning fish.

There are whales in these waters, whales with hearts the size of cars and heartbeats loud enough to be heard two miles away. Naked in the gray water, the bride goes under and listens for whale heartbeats. They find her there. They give her tea, put her to bed, swath her in white, place lilies in her hand, and send her down the aisle toward an altar framed by two slender white-barked trees.

6

I decide that I should like to be married in a straw hat, a straw hat so huge it verges on the ridiculous, and a long red dress with scenes of Japanese tea gardens printed all over it in white, and a pair of large green hoop earrings, and a pair of rhinestone shoes bought on the beach in Los Angeles, and enormous sunglasses with rims the color of Coca-Cola.

I am sorry, but this is simply what I want to wear when I am married. I refuse to wear anything else. So: I must go out and find these items. But not a single store in New York City has a straw hat as huge as the straw hat in my imagination. Why, why, why, does this always happen? Reality lags so very far behind everything else.

A long red dress with scenes of Japanese tea gardens printed all over it in white? No such luck. There aren't any hoop earrings in the particular grassy shade of green I envision. I live 2,793 miles away from the beach in Los Angeles where they sell rhinestone shoes. And, of course, no sunglasses are as much like Coca-Cola as the sunglasses I desire.

Exhausted from marching around in the obscene murky heat of June, from visiting every single store in New York City, from the music these stores play to manipulate the unmanipulatable imaginations of patrons such as myself, I walk back to the cottage where he and I live. The rooms smell of rosemary cooking in olive oil. He is nowhere to be seen. Laid out on the bed is a straw hat; a long red dress; a pair of hoop earrings; a pair of rhinestone shoes; a pair of sunglasses. A confession: none of these objects is quite perfect, none of them aligns flawlessly with the picture in my head—yet suddenly my imagination reshapes itself around these new objects, the objects he has gathered, and now these objects are precisely what I have been thinking of all along.

7

Because of everything that's happened, they're forced to settle in a small square suburban house. Adam, driven by natural instinct, tends the lawn. He even figures out the lawnmower. Eve, however, almost burns the house down when she attempts to use the stove. She declares she won't eat anything until she can eat fruit right off trees in their own yard. There are no trees at all in their yard, much less any fruit trees. Quickly, they learn the difference between making love and fucking. Afterward, Eve cries. She walks through the rooms, recalling the clean golden light of the other place. Here, the air is velvety with car exhaust.

Much to their surprise, Eve has a baby. They didn't know anything about anything. They'd assumed she was getting fat from all the potato chips he bought at the gas station since she refused to cook. But then one day she starts to feel large, dangerous things happening in her gut. Adam is still a slow and nervous driver; by the time they get to the hospital, the upholstery is soaked with Eve's blood.

They do the things they're supposed to do. They send their sons to school. Eve learns how to cook, and how to operate the dishwasher. She buys makeup. Adam works as a landscaper. He wears a baseball cap. They have their neighbors over for barbecues. They take photographs of their sons on prom night. Eve develops heavy jowls and sharply plucked eyebrows. She dyes her hair dark brown, almost black. She learns how to laugh heartily, prefers jellied fruit to raw.

One evening, the sunset in the suburbs is uncharacteristically golden.

"Hey," Adam says when Eve hands him a beer, "does this remind you of anything?"

"Honey," she says, "that goddamn dryer isn't—"

"Doesn't this remind you of anything?"

"Sure, baby," she says, "it reminds me of a nice sunset." There's nothing else it could remind her of, because she was born and raised in the suburbs, and this is all she's ever known.

8

Once you've been dead for a period of time, you know how true it is that we each die alone; and indeed Snow White remained vaguely cognizant of this truth even after her life had revived and resolved itself in joyous ways…

She and Prince X were a happy couple. (In fact, everyone found them infuriatingly darling, and whenever they were paraded through the streets, the roses tossed upon them contained, tucked among their petals, small cryptic curses—"Sixteen onions in a barrel of brine, You may be hers but *she* is *mine!*" Obviously the royal couple never saw these; only the hunchbacked, dwarfish street sweepers read them, giggling strangely.) They were happy…but Prince X was a dreamy fellow and sometimes vanished into his imagination, leaving her alone with her knowledge that we each die alone. She searched for him in dusty abandoned towers. Speculating that perhaps he had been magically shrunken, she hunted for him in the sugar bowl.

By the time he reappeared, barging through the bronze doors and proposing a picnic on the parapet, she'd already become lost in solitude. She wondered if the huntsman had removed her heart and replaced it with a clump of frozen dirt. What else could explain this terrible coldness in her, this immunity to his eager eyes? How she wished she could coo back at him! But we each die alone! "Polgi nitsway," she said apologetically. "Ogblitefa?"

"What a joker you are!" he exclaimed, embracing her.

"Ikne faldig ti!" She squirmed away and ran to the mirror. She was herself—black hair! pure skin! red lips!—and yet she was not. "Folea badong, u lemrig!" It was no joke—this had become the only language she knew. Her solitude swelled and completed itself. For days she'd live lonesomely at his side, her heart like a tin can and her mouth producing only unrecognizable words. Eventually, her mind would wrap itself around his language again.

ALPHABETS OF SAND

Marilyn Hacker and Deema Shehabi

The French poet and
the Egyptian novelist
walked on stage to read.

Twelve armed cops broke down the door
(unlocked). So Jerusalem's

Palestinian
literary festival
was displaced, to a

diplomat's garden. Nor was
this an Egyptian movie...

> Many decades ago,
> the Russian novelist said
> to close the heart of a country

> is to shut down its literature,
> but the peasant still says:

> let's cut this cloth
> against the body of tyranny
> and embroider our free symbols:

> hoopoe, cypress,
> anemones and zaytun

Marilyn Hacker received the 2010 PEN/Voelcker Award for Poetry. The poems here make up a renga, a Japanese form in which two poets respond to one another. The indented stanzas are by Deema Shehabi.

Olives like pebbles
fell on the tarpaulin
spread under the trees.

We stood on ladders, plucking,
joking, were pelted with rain,

then sat by the fire
drinking arak, arguing
about resistance,

Akhmatova and Darwish
—olives to the press next day.

*

Rabeea grinned and said
« No offense to the Aunties,
but putting us out here in the shack

without asking us was a
bad idea. » Rahma, Jannan,

Zohra, and Hanna nodded
in agreement as the thick fog
stiffened outside our window.

We turned to the helping
verbs, the scent of chicken feathers in the air—

When the worst recedes,
the night soldiers' wreckage,
the boy with the knife,

there are verbs to conjugate,
grammar books' bland sentences

in which a young man
gets off a train; a schoolgirl
runs to catch a bus,

the ruptured world composes
yumkininî ân. I might.

*

"Come share my meal," said
the poet to the red wolf
in desert firelight.

Fangs glistened in the flames,
and a honed sword set aside.

The wolf was hungry,
accustomed to betrayals.
The man offered food

and a truce. What happened next,
neither wolf nor poet told.

*

The days were waterless,
and the nights engorged
with clouds—

the meal was a handful
of nuts, grapes, and dates,

like on the old caravans
to Mecca. He tired often
and slept restlessly

beneath the musk of her
hair: one half vanilla-clove,

A cinnamon clove,
a mollusk sheathing a pearl,
a wild strawberry,

humble hidden savory

engorged with a mother tongue,

not the origin
of the world, hell's mouth, flood-rift,
blind spot in the sea.

What are you talking about?
Irrelevant metaphors.

    *

    You spill the chai
    on the rug at the eid prayer.
    The women pour in—dressed

    in orange and turquoise saris.
    Faint coconut oil on black hair.

    This one is called Ayeshah,
    and she calls you sister.
    On the big screen, the imam says

    You reach hell's mouth
    when you keep getting into debt.

He got into debt:
the boy's fees for private school,
after that, the girl's

but a goldsmith made a good
living… Journalist? Doctor?

His daughter watches
videos between blackouts,
afraid to go out.

No news from the boy since he
took that van toward the border.

    Between blackouts,
    he watches videos of

Grease, temporarily suspended
in Olivia Newton John's innocence
lost. Before magreb, he'd peek

out at the soldiers
from the living room curtains,
amazed at how these streets

where he used to fly down with his
dirt bike are now filled with tanks—

What grabbed at his gut
turning the corner under
polleny lindens

on a summer morning as
brightly dressed women headed

to market, what made
the broad street a dark staircase
(while sun tagged boys' bikes),

his impatience, vertigo
was, he recognized it, fear.

*

This letter, witty,
flirtatious: six names for *horse*
from the Omeyyads.

This one from elsewhere: they shot
a teacher in the street, left

the body to be
defiled. A border apart,
on her desk today.

She begs her not to despair.
Copies the six words for *horse*.

At the funeral, she weeps
at the despair in the eyes
of Leila's boys. She studies the photos:

a youthful Leila in New York
with black, shiny hair. Another one

taken at the mouth
of a Syrian holy cave known
for curing miracles,

her head covered with a stylish red cap,
the summer before she died.

A brown wool knit cap
pulled over her pony-tail,
she read elegies

in translation. On the screen
Baghdad burned again, again.

Another teacher
in rose silk shalwar qameez
came up and hugged her;

they called each other sister
in their adopted language.

Sitting upright in a Tel Aviv
hospital bed, he composes
elegies to his departed mother:

The dawn nursed her face,
honey colored until the day—

He looks up to see Arwa
entering the room,
her hand on her cheek.

He smiles at her: Ahlan yakhti,
Why is there sadness in your eyes?

Oh moon, my sister
has shrapnel lodged in her skull.
She is nine years old.

They shot our father and our
small brother in the doorway.

Her name is Amal,
or Hope, she lay for three days
under the rubble.

When she cries out in her sleep
I do not think about peace.

*

*Was he shedding tears
of remorse, or longing for
that other city?*

Cavafy might have written
transposing Byzantium.

"Go to the doctor,
yâ waladî, that looks like
conjunctivitis."

—keeping his hands to himself,
like the Alexandrian.

Darwish could no longer rise
from his bed to meet the beloved.
He was always longing

for that other city,
city of weeping guitars,

of Gacelas and wise lizards
who hold secrets of bitter roots
in their sewn-up mouths.

Sometimes, he could still hear the shots
that killed him, the gypsy poet of green rain—

Cloud cuneiforms,
the calligraphy of rain,
alphabets of sand

slip through her fingers as the
old woman copies the words

of a couplet by
Abu al-'Atahiyya
"Death is certain yet

I am still joyful, as if
I knew death through denial."

MOTHER TONGUE

LILA AZAM ZANGANEH: Atiq, you wrote three novels in Persian, and then you switched from Persian to French for your most recent novel, *The Patience Stone*, and it went on to win the Prix Goncourt, France's most prestigious literary prize. The novel is called *The Patience Stone*, which is the name of a stone from—is this an Islamic tradition?

ATIQ RAHIMI: No, it exists only in Afghanistan, Iran, and Tajikistan.

ZANGANEH: And what is the Patience Stone, the Sang-E Saboor?

RAHIMI: It is a legendary and magical stone. You have to put it in front of you, and then you can talk to it and express all of your suffering and your secrets. The stone will listen and absorb all of this. One day it will explode, and on that day you will finally be freed of all of that suffering.

ZANGANEH: And is that day the day of the apocalypse? The female character in the book says it might be. Is that a common thought?

RAHIMI: No, that's just my idea. It's a literary device that I use.

ZANGANEH: At the very beginning of *The Patience Stone* you have an epigraph by Antonin Artaud: "From the body by the body with the body / Since the body and until the body." This idea of lending a body and a textured voice to an Afghan woman is really at the heart of your literary endeavor here. Let me read one page to give a sense of the work and exactly what that means— because there is nothing more taboo in Afghanistan than talking about a woman in terms of her sex and sexuality.

> "I lived with your name. I had never seen, or heard, or touched you
> before that day. I was afraid, afraid of everything, of you, of going to

This transcript was adapted from a conversation that took place at the 2010 PEN World Voices Festival. Atiq Rahimi spoke in French, and his words were interpreted by Lilia Pino-Blouin.

bed, of the blood. But at the same time, it was a fear I enjoyed. You know, the kind of fear that doesn't separate you from your desire, but instead arouses you, gives you wings, even though it may burn. That was the kind of fear I was feeling. And it was growing in me every day, invading my belly, my guts… On the night before you arrived, it came pouring out. It wasn't a blue fear. No. It was a red fear, blood red. When I mentioned it to my aunt, she advised me not to say anything… and so I kept quiet. That suited me fine. Although I was a virgin I was really scared. I kept wondering what would happen if by any chance I didn't bleed that night…" Her hand sweeps through the air as if batting away a fly. "It would have been a catastrophe. I'd heard so many stories about that. I could imagine the whole thing." Her voice becomes mocking. "Passing off impure blood as virginal blood, bit of a brainwave, don't you think?" She lies down right close to the man. "I have never understood why, for you men, pride is so much linked to blood." Her hand sweeps the air again. Her fingers are moving. As if gesturing to an invisible person to come closer. "And remember the night—it was when we were first living together—that you came home late. Dead drunk. You'd been smoking. I had fallen asleep. You pulled down my knickers without saying a word. I woke up. But I pretended to be deeply asleep. You… penetrated me… you had a great time… but when you stood up to go and wash yourself you noticed blood on your dick. You were furious. You came back and beat me, in the middle of the night, just because I hadn't warned you that I was bleeding. I had defiled you!" She laughs, scornful. "I had made you unclean." Her hand snatches memories from the air, closes around them, descends to stroke her belly as it swells and slackens at a pace faster than the man's breathing.

Suddenly, she thrusts her hands downward, beneath her dress, between her legs. Closes her eyes. Takes a deep, ragged breath. Rams her fingers into herself, roughly, as if driving in a blade. Holding her breath, she pulls out her hand with a stifled cry. Opens her eyes and looks at the tips of her nails. They are wet. Wet with blood. Red with blood. She puts her hand in front of the man's vacant eyes. "Look! That's my blood, too. Clean. What's the difference between menstrual blood and blood that is clean? What's so disgusting about this blood?" Her hand moves down to the man's nostrils. "You were born of this blood! It is cleaner than the blood of your own body!" She pushes her fingers roughly into his beard. As she brushes his lips she feels his breath. A shiver of fear runs across her skin. Her arm shudders. She pulls her hand away, clenches her fist, and, with her mouth against the pillow, cries out again. Just once. The cry is long. Heartrending. She doesn't move for a long time. A very long time. Until the water bearer knocks on the neighbor's door, and the old woman's rasping cough is heard through the walls, and the water bearer empties his skin into the neighbor's tank, and one of her daughters starts crying in the passage. Then, she stands up and leaves the room without daring to look at her man.

So many things are contained in this passage that I'd love to talk about, but first I want to ask about the language. You have said in interviews that it would have been impossible to write this book in Persian. You wrote your first three books in Persian, and you said those books had a kind of self-censorship, because of what could not be said in Persian. What was the first little throb, the first impulse, to change the language of your own writing?

RAHIMI: I must admit that I actually never wanted to write in French. I still feel that way. I feel that I can write a screenplay or an article in French, but as far as literature is concerned, as far as a text that is full of your own emotions, your own feelings—something so personal, so intimate—I think it is important to write in your own language, your own "mother tongue." The language you use when you cry, when you laugh. The language you use to understand the world. But in this specific case, the very first sentence just came out in French. After that first sentence I wanted to change to Persian, but I soon found out I was incapable, so I stopped trying. I started writing in French, and then the words came easily to me—the story itself seemed to guide me. Now that the book is done and published, I have some distance and I can think about what happened—and I realize now that one's mother tongue is not suitable for writing something of this kind. Just think of the term itself: "mother tongue." There is something about it that makes it unsuitable for this subject matter. There is some kind of modesty, some reserve.

ZANGANEH: The book tells the story of a woman whose man—they don't have names—has taken a bullet in the neck and is lying in a coma. She doesn't know if he can hear anything or not, but he has an open mouth and a tube that feeds him water and salt. Because he can't talk, *she* begins to talk for the first time, she begins to empty out her heart and tell him about her own pain and what she has endured. Then she becomes more and more bold, in a sense. She talks about everything from the most outrageous secrets of her life to the tiniest thing—that she hasn't been able to kiss him, for instance.

"To kiss him in the way that I see in those Indian movies," she says, which is a wonderful line. She says: *We've never touched, you've never listened to me.* You give voice to this woman and her intimate life—and it is impossible for me to imagine this in Persian. Would it have been possible? The book was translated into Persian and was published in Iran. How would you go about writing this in Persian?

RAHIMI: After the book was published I was asked multiple times to translate it myself into Persian—and I did try, but it just did not work. Then, all of a sudden, I got a call and someone told me it had been published in Iran. And of course many passages had been censored. I must say, in terms of the language, the translation is not very well done. But what I find shocking is that, in spite of the fact that many passages were cut, others I would have expected to be—for example, the one that you read—were not. In the passage you read, some words were cut; for "sex," they put in three dots. But they basically revealed what it is, because we know what would have been there. I just don't understand the resistance in our countries to talking about these things. When you go back to classical literature—think of Rumi, he named "sex" straight out. There is a book, *Masnavi,* which has a passage that is almost pornographic. It's the story of a merchant who leaves his wife home alone, and he has a parrot that is supposed to tell him if the wife cheats. There are all these temptations; people try to have sex with her. In 1998, I was in Tehran and I found Kundera's book *The Unbearable Lightness of Being,* and I wondered, "How could such a book be translated into Persian?" So I bought it and started reading. And it was surreal: all the passages between Tomas and Tereza, where Tereza is his lover, well, she was changed into his sister. I thought, "Maybe the young soldier who falls in love with my character will be turned into her brother." That would make it incestuous and perverted.

ZANGANEH: We were talking a few days ago and you said that one of the defining characteristics of our cultural era and our region is that somewhere along the line the body was canceled out. And literature, the texture of literature, is an allegory for the body having been canceled out. We have lost that—and as a writer you're trying to bring back the body. How did that happen, do you think?

RAHIMI: I was always shocked by this distance in our culture between the body and the mind. In classical Persian poetry, even in mystical poetry, we find something extraordinary—that, as far as I know, only exists in Persian; I haven't found it in any other language. I'm talking about one specific word, "jaan." You, as an Iranian woman, would know about this. It's a word that is used in Iran and Afghanistan and Tajikistan. It is a word of daily life. It's something that we add to the name: for example, you would be Lilajaan. It would be translated as "my dear Lila." It is a word that describes at the same time the body and the soul. There is no separation in "jaan." This separation is something that we find in Christian culture, in Judaism, and in Islam, but before that we had this idea. The separation came about with Islam and with the Judeo-Christian tradition; in our language, we say the word "jessm" for body and "rooh" for soul. But these words are not Persian words, we borrowed them from Arabic. So if we go back to mystic poets—I always like going back to Rumi; he uses this word with its full ambiguity. I could mention hundreds of poems by Rumi where he uses this word. And if you interpret "jaan" as "rooh," or soul, then you have a very mystical poem. But if you interpret it as "body," then they become erotic poems.

ZANGANEH: In a sense, in Persian literature, the seventeenth century begins a hiatus, and then in the twentieth century a tradition begins again. You've differentiated between the subcontinent and our cultural region. In India, the body has remained, it exists, it continues to thrive. But ours has disappeared, not just from literature, but slowly it has disappeared from the body politic, so to speak, as well. What happened?

RAHIMI: That's a long story, politically speaking. As you said, starting in the seventeenth or the eighteenth century this gap formed between the Western world and our region. In those centuries the West started opening to the world—and conquering the world. Up to that point, the East had been open to the world as well. There had been study of Aristotle and Plato. But at that point in the seventeenth or eighteenth century, the Orient needed to protect itself, and so it closed itself to that experience. The Muslim world wasn't able to follow and did not participate in what was happening—and that's when this detachment, this gap, was created. Poets, artists, and intellectuals who were from the Persian or Islamic area were just left behind. As the great Iranian philosopher Dariush Shayegan said, we have a "mutilated" look. A mental distortion was created in Persian and Muslim society. That gave rise to this new voice that has guided our culture. I must point out that Islam developed differently in Iran and Afghanistan and Tajikistan than in Arab-speaking countries. Actually, when Islam arrived in our region it found two big religions already present. One of them was Buddhism and the other was Zoroastrianism. Islam did not impose itself on these traditions, but rather superimposed itself on them. So what was created was a mix of Buddhist and Zoroastrian elements that were integrated into this form of Islam.

ZANGANEH: It reminds me of Hegel, when he talks about reason and history, and specifically the French Revolution. He's trying to explain the extraordinary violence of the French Revolution. He says that when a people or a government tries to implement abstract universal ideas, concrete individuals will come in the way and that's where violence and terror occur. The government is trying to implement an abstract universal, but of course things will never fall into place. Some people will be more equal than others, and, at some point we'll have to cut off heads. And this affair of the body I find quite enlightening, because we tried to establish in Iran, with the revolution, and in Afghanistan, this abstract universal idea of a sexless society, which was highly regimented and where sex disappeared from the public space. And then, of course, every time sex sprang up its head had to be cut off. Then you arrive: a man who lived in Afghanistan for about a third of his life, and, at the age of forty-five, is now living in France. And you lend a body and a voice, through your work, not only to a woman, but to a literary tradition. At this point we begin to see the political import of your work. The political impetus begins to inhabit your language in a way that gives it a very particular texture. What gave you the first inkling, the first desire, to inhabit, in your writing, the body of a woman?

RAHIMI: You mentioned the poem by Artaud earlier. That really is the program for this book. This book is focused on the body—and I found three dimensions to this body. In the beginning the woman has no body, she is ashamed of her body, and the man, his body, is lying there as a stone. He is on the floor, he doesn't move, he has no desires. Both bodies, of the man and of the woman, are objects of suffering, elements of shame. And this is something in all the main monotheistic religions—the body is always associated with shame, something that should be rejected, something that has an expiration date and will go back to the earth. In the beginning of the novel, this is the form that the body takes. The second stage is when the woman is obliged to become a prostitute. At that point, the body becomes an object of commerce. Something that can be sold, and this is what happens, of course, in many countries. It no longer brings shame, but rather a trade.

ZANGANEH: There is an interesting moment in the book when the woman needs to lie. She says to someone who invades the house, "I am a prostitute." She says this to save herself, because she knows that if she doesn't tell him that she's a prostitute—which is a lie at the time—she will be raped. She says, "Prostitutes are worthless." Because, in fact, in prostitution, in the Islamic context, the woman is not dominated; it is a relationship of exchange. I thought that that was extremely interesting.

RAHIMI: Little by little throughout the book this young woman gets to know a soldier and they fall in love. She becomes his lover—and at that point the body is no longer something to be ashamed of or something to be sold. It is no longer an object. It becomes a subject. She becomes conscious of her body and her soul becomes part of her body. Her soul is nowhere else but in her body. It's like a sheet where one side is the body and one side is the soul, but it is one single thing. We arrive to this beautiful idea where the body and the mind are just one magnificent, symbiotic element; there isn't the cult of the body over the cult of the soul, there isn't a prominence of one over the other, they are just one beautiful thing. In terms of religion, the woman starts seeing herself as a prophet. She develops her own religion, which is not a religion of the soul or of the body, but is in fact a religion of the jaan.

ZANGANEH: In the end she says, "I am revealed." It's a moment of ecstasy almost; it's a very mystical moment. It parallels a crescendo in the dramatic tension—she talks about the Sang-E Saboor, the Patience Stone. She imagines the moment the Patience Stone explodes as the apocalypse, and of course apocalypse, in Greek, means revelation. So all of this is leads to a moment of revelation where she says, "I am revealed." It's a harrowing moment. Before we open this up to the audience, I wonder if you could talk about the end of the book and what it might lead to.

RAHIMI: There are two things. First of all, I can't really say what will happen in terms of the reality of our world. I don't think we're close to having found the solution for these things. At a personal level, my hope is that humankind can move towards this idea of jaan, just like this woman at the end of the book who is revealed. She finds grace through the body in a way that allows her to also include her soul and vice versa. She fully accomplishes this idea of jaan. I hope that that's where we can all move as societies. It's a matter of beginning this consciousness. I think in the next fifty or one hundred years we will get there. I hope so.

ZANGANEH: On that hopeful note, let's open this up to the audience.

AUDIENCE: Was your book censored in Afghanistan, Saudi Arabia, or through Al-Azhar in Cairo?

RAHIMI: My book has not been translated into Arabic yet, but it has been distributed in French in Arab-speaking countries. I have actually traveled to Morocco and to Tunisia to present it. As far as Saudi Arabia is concerned, I don't think it will ever be distributed there. As far as I see it, Saudi Arabia is tantamount to the Taliban regime right now.

AUDIENCE: In 2008, you received the Prix Goncourt, and the cultural institutions of France gave official recognition to an Afghan exile. Just a few months after this accomplishment, the same government closed down some Afghan refugee camps in France. Those were two things that went in opposite directions. What do you think about that?

RAHIMI: The very day after I was awarded the Prix Goncourt, the French government prepared a charter to send back Afghan refugees. It wasn't a few months after; it was really the very day after. And I issued a formal declaration in which I condemned this policy and I formally asked the government to cancel this initiative, which they did. A few months later, with the help of Great Britain, they did send back these refugees. Personally, I am very active in fighting against such measures and promoting the rights of political refugees—not only Afghan ones. Of course it is a very complicated issue; it isn't easy to solve. I don't think that the E.U. or France should just accept every refugee without any regulation, but I am very involved in trying to improve their conditions. In particular, I work a lot with young people. If there is any hope to save Afghanistan, it must come from young people who stay in Afghanistan and rebuild their country from the inside. My generation is already done for. It's already corrupt. If we want to have a future, what we need to work on is education, on culture, with our young people. So I prefer to work inside Afghanistan. Of course, when I see people from Afghanistan in Paris, I feel close to them, but that's more of a humanitarian type of attitude, whereas I believe in humanism more.

ZANGANEH: Atiq, you went back to Afghanistan one month after the start of the war.

RAHIMI: In January, yes. The first of January, 2002.

ZANGANEH: You went back for the first time in eighteen years. You helped create writers' workshops, you helped young filmmakers, people involved in media. Perhaps that's the revelation we were talking about. I'm assuming there are women in your workshops as well.

RAHIMI: Of course.

AUDIENCE: How have you been received in Afghanistan? And what was the response in Iran to the bad translation?

RAHIMI: When I got the Prix Goncourt, there was a caricature that was published in a French magazine. It showed Afghan women in burqas. They were talking and one said, "You know, Atiq won this prestigious prize." And the other said, "Yeah, great, thank God our husbands don't know what the book is about." My book does tackle all kinds of issues, which Lila analyzed brilliantly, and it does take risks. Personally, I believe that if I can't wake people up, I'll at least make their sleep troubled. In Iran, nobody talks about the book. There is silence. I don't know if it's out of fear that they can't talk about it, or if it's worse than that. Somebody did write something about the book on the internet, and their point was that if this book was published in Iran, it would allow you to see where freedom will take women.

AUDIENCE: Do you believe that social change and the democratic process should materialize from within a country, or do you believe foreign assistance is warranted? And would you advocate the immediate ending of the intervention of Western powers in Afghanistan?

RAHIMI: It's a huge question. Of course we cannot impose democracy using military force; it is a contradiction in terms. But on the other hand, democracy never happened without violence. We tend to forget that the West paid very hard and for a long time for the democracy that it has now. Without revolutions and wars, the West would not enjoy this democracy. If you think about it, democracy started in ancient Greece—but then there were centuries of the Dark Ages, of total silence for democracy, up until the eighteenth century. And even the United States, the land of democracy, had to pay hard and make great sacrifices for that. Freedom and peace demand great sacrifices, unfortunately. This is intrinsic to the logic of power. Human beings are not angels.

AUDIENCE: The French government is trying to say that students cannot wear burqas. Do you support that law?

RAHIMI: In my own country I fight against the veil, so how could I ever support it in France? On the other hand, I think that this issue in a country such as France is almost a trick. It becomes a political debate. The idea is that on the one hand, if you want to be democratic, every person has the right to express her religion, her individuality, so she should be allowed to wear the veil if that's what she wants. So if you make it illegal, you are using a democratic law to impose something which becomes an obligation and no longer allows the individual to make a choice, so that becomes a contradiction in society. Another point that people make is that when Western people go to Iran they have to observe the dress code there, so why should we in the West allow Muslims to do whatever they want in Western countries? But if you follow that same logic then the French government is on the same level as the Iranian government. I think this is not the debate we should be having. Obviously the veil issue is very charged, very political. My belief is that it is not with laws that we can give freedom to women who are imprisoned now. In my view, that freedom will come from culture and from education, in France and everywhere else.

FICTION

THE ART OF DEALING WITH GENIUSES

Amélie Nothomb

Translated by Alison Anderson

"Monsieur Tach, before anything else, on behalf of my entire profession I would like to apologize for what happened yesterday."

"What is supposed to have happened yesterday?"

"Well, that journalist dishonored us, bothering you the way he did."

"Ah yes, I remember. A very nice boy. When will I see him again?"

"Never again, rest assured. You might like to know he's sick as a dog today."

"Poor boy! What happened?"

"Too many egg flips."

"I've always known that egg flips can play dirty tricks on you. If I had been aware of his taste for such invigorating beverages, I would have mixed him a good Brandy Alexander, there's nothing like it for the metabolism. Would you like a Brandy Alexander, young man?"

"Never while I'm on duty, thank you."

The journalist failed to notice the intensely suspicious gaze that his refusal inspired.

"Monsieur Tach, you must not be angry with our colleague over what happened yesterday. There are not many journalists who have been properly trained to meet individuals like yourself…"

"That's all we need. Train good people so they can meet me! You could call such a discipline 'The art of dealing with geniuses!' How dreadful!"

"Don't you think? May I conclude that you won't hold it against my colleague? Thank you for your understanding."

"Have you come here to talk about your colleague, or to talk about me?"

"About you, of course, this was just by way of introduction."

"What a pity. Dear Lord, the prospect is so distressing that I need a Brandy Alexander. I hope you don't mind waiting a moment—it's your fault, after all, you shouldn't have mentioned Brandy Alexanders, you've made me want one with all your carrying on."

"But I never said anything about Brandy Alexanders!"

"Don't be in bad faith, young man. I cannot stand bad faith. You still don't want to taste my beverage?"

He did not realize that Tach was offering him his last chance, and he let it slip by. Shrugging his huge shoulders, the novelist wheeled his chair over toward a sort of coffin, then raised the lid, revealing bottles, cans of food, and tankards.

"This is a Merovingian coffin," explained the fat man, "that I've converted into a bar."

He took hold of one of three big metal goblets, poured a generous dose of crème de cacao, and some brandy. He gave the journalist a cunning glance.

"And now, you're going to learn the chef's secret. The common of mortals adds a final third of heavy cream. I think that's a bit too rich, so I've replaced the cream by an equivalent amount of… (he grabbed hold of one on the cans) sweet condensed milk." (And went on to illustrate his words with his gesture.)

"But that must be disgustingly rich!" said the journalist, sinking deeper.

"This year, we're having a mild winter. When it's cold, I add a big dollop of melted butter to my Brandy Alexander."

"I beg your pardon?"

"Yes. Condensed milk does not contain as much fat as cream, so you have to make up for it. In fact, as it is still only January 15, theoretically I am entitled to add some butter, but to do so I would have to go into the kitchen and leave you alone, and that would be ill-mannered. So I will do without the butter."

"Please, I beg you, don't deprive yourself for my sake."

"No, never mind. In honor of the ultimatum that expires this evening, I shall do without butter."

"Do you feel directly concerned by the Gulf crisis?"

"So concerned that I am not adding butter to my Brandy Alexander."

"Do you follow the news on television?"

"Between commercial breaks, I sometimes subject myself to the news."

"What do you think of the Gulf crisis?"

"Nothing."

"You still think nothing?"

"Nothing."

"You're completely indifferent to it?"

"Not at all. But what I might think about it is irrelevant. You shouldn't ask a fat man for his opinion on this crisis. I am neither a general, nor a pacifist, nor a gas station attendant, nor an Iraqi. However, if you ask me about Brandy Alexanders, I shall be brilliant."

To conclude his flight of eloquence, the novelist raised the tankard to his lips and quaffed a few gluttonous gulps.

"Why do you drink from a metal container?"

"I don't like transparency. That is also one of the reasons why I am so fat: I don't like for people to see through me."

"Speaking of which, Monsieur Tach, I would like to ask you something that all the journalists are burning to ask, but have never dared."

"How much I weigh?"

"No, what you eat. We know that food is a very important part of your life. Gastronomy, and its natural consequence, digestion, are at the heart of some of your recent novels such as *An Apology for Dyspepsia*, a work which, to me, seems to contain a condensed version of your metaphysical concerns."

"Exactly. I consider metaphysics to be the best form of expression for the metabolism. Along the same line, since one's metabolism can be divided into anabolism and catabolism, I have split metaphysics into anaphysics and cataphysics. This should not be seen as a dualist tension, but as two obligatory and, more inconveniently, simultaneous phases of a thought process devoted to triviality."

"Is this not also an allusion to Jarry and pataphysics?"

"No, monsieur. *I* am a *serious* writer," answered the old man icily, before imbibing another swallow of Brandy Alexander.

"So, Monsieur Tach, if you please, would you be so kind as to outline for me the various digestive stages in a typical day of your life?"

There was a solemn silence, while the novelist seemed to be thinking. Then he began to speak, in a grave tone of voice, as if he were unveiling some secret dogma.

"In the morning, I wake up at around eight o'clock. I go to the toilet to empty my bladder and my intestines. Would you like any details?"

"No, I think that should be enough."

"So much the better, because while it is an indispensable stage in the digestive process, it is absolutely disgusting, that you may believe."

"I'll take your word for it."

"Blessed are they who have not seen and yet have believed. After that, I powder myself, then I get dressed."

"Do you always wear this dressing gown?"

"Yes, except when I go out shopping."

"Does your handicap not make it difficult to get around?"

"I've had time to get used to it. Then I go into the kitchen and make my breakfast. In the old days, when I spent my time writing, I didn't cook, and I ate coarse meals, such as cold tripe..."

"Cold tripe in the morning?"

"I can see why you might be surprised. You must realize that in those days, writing was virtually my sole preoccupation. But nowadays I would find it repulsive to eat cold tripe in the morning. For twenty years I have been in the habit of browning it in goose fat for half an hour."

"Tripe in goose fat for breakfast?"

"It's excellent."

"And you have a Brandy Alexander with that?"

"No, never when I eat. Back in the days when I was writing, I drank strong coffee. Nowadays I prefer eggnog. After that, I go out shopping and spend my morning cooking up a refined dish for lunch: fritters of brain, kidneys en daube…"

"And complicated desserts?"

"Rarely. I drink only sweet things, so I don't really feel like dessert. The occasional toffee between meals. When I was young, I preferred Scottish toffees, which are exceptionally hard. Alas, with age, I now have to make do with soft toffees, which are excellent nonetheless. I venture to claim that nothing can equal the voluptuous sensation of being bogged down that is concomitant with the paralysis of one's jaws caused by chewing English toffees… Do write down what I just said, I think it rings rather well."

"There's no need, it's all being recorded."

"What? That's dishonest! I can't say anything foolish, in other words?"

"You never say anything foolish, Monsieur Tach."

"You are as flattering as a sycophant, Monsieur."

"Please, do go on with your digestive stations of the Cross."

"My digestive stations of the Cross? That's a good one. You didn't steal it from one of my novels by any chance?"

"No, I made it up."

"That would surprise me. I would swear it was Prétextat Tach. There was a time when I knew my works by heart… Alas, we are as old as our memory, don't you agree? And it's not the arteries, as some imbeciles would have it. Let's see, 'digestive stations of the Cross,' where did I write that?"

"Monsieur Tach, even if you had written it, I would be just as deserving for saying it, given that—"

The journalist came to a sudden stop, biting his lips.

"—given that you've never read a thing I've written, have you? Thank you, young man, that's all I wanted to know. Who are you to believe such boundless twaddle? Do you honestly think I would ever make up such a flashy, mediocre expression as 'digestive stations of the Cross'? It's just about worthy of a second-rate theologian like yourself. Well, I can see with a somewhat senile sense of relief that the literary world has not changed: It is still the triumph of those who pretend to have read What's-his-name. However, in your day and age, there is nothing deserving about that: Nowadays, you can buy so-called study guides that enable illiterate people to talk about great authors with every appearance of an average culture. And this is where you are mistaken: I consider the fact someone has not read me to be most deserving. I would have warm admiration for a journalist who came to interview me without even knowing who I am, and who would not hide his ignorance. But if what you know is on the order of a powdered milk shake—'Add water for a ready-to-drink milkshake'—can you imagine anything more mediocre?"

"Try to understand. Today is the fifteenth, and the news about your cancer was announced on the tenth. You have already published twenty-two major novels, it would have been impossible to read them in so little time, particularly in these turbulent days when we are all focused on the latest news from the Middle East."

"The Gulf crisis is more interesting than my corpse, I'll grant you that. But the time you spent cramming with the help of those study guides would have been better spent reading even just ten pages from one of my books."

"I have something to confess."

"There is no need, I understand: You tried, and you gave up before you had even reached page ten, is that it? I guessed as much, the moment I saw you. I can recognize instantaneously the people who have read me: You can see it on their face. But you looked neither upset, nor bright, nor fat, nor thin, nor ecstatic: You looked healthy. So you haven't read any more of me than your colleague from yesterday. And that is why, in spite of everything, I still find you somewhat to my liking. All the more so in that you gave up before page ten: That is proof of a strength of character I have never been capable of. Moreover, your attempt to confess—superfluous—does you credit. In fact, I would have disliked you immensely if you had well and truly read me, and were just as I see you now. But that is enough laughable conjecture. We were talking about my digestion, if my memory serves me correctly?"

"That's right. Talking about toffees, to be exact."

"Well, when I have finished lunch, I head for the smoking room. This is one of the high points of the day. I can only tolerate your interviews in the morning, because in the afternoon, I smoke until five o'clock."

"Why five o'clock?"

"At five o'clock this stupid nurse arrives, who thinks it's useful to bathe me from head to toe: yet another one of Gravelin's ideas. A daily bath, can you imagine? Vanitas vanitum sed omnia vanitas. So I take my revenge however I can, I find a way to stink as much as I can, so as to inconvenience that innocent young thing, I garnish my lunch with entire heads of garlic, I invent all sorts of circulatory ailments, and then I smoke like a Turk until the intrusion of my washerwoman."

He gave a hideous laugh.

"Don't tell me you smoke like that with the sole intention of asphyxiating the unfortunate woman?"

"That would be reason enough, but the truth is that I adore smoking cigars. If I didn't choose to smoke at that time, there would be nothing pernicious about the activity—I insist on the word activity, because for me, smoking is an activity in its own right, and I can tolerate no visits or distractions while I'm smoking."

"This is very interesting, Monsieur Tach, but let's not get off the subject: Your cigars have nothing to do with your digestion."

"You don't think so? I'm not so sure. Well, if it doesn't interest you... And my bath, are you interested in that?"

"No, unless you eat the soap or drink the bath water."

"Can you imagine, that bitch has me get naked, then she scrubs my spare tires, and showers my hindquarters? I'm sure it gives her an orgasm, just to be soaking a naked, hairless, crippled fat man. Those nurses are all obsessed. That's why they go into such a filthy profession."

"Monsieur Tach, I believe we are getting off the subject again..."

"I don't agree. This daily episode is so perverse that it upsets my digestion. Can you imagine! I'm all alone, humiliated, monstrously fat, and as naked as a worm in the bathwater, in the presence of this clothed creature who undresses me every day, wearing her hypocritically professional expression to hide the fact that she's wetting her underpants—if the bitch is even wearing any—and when she goes back to the hospital, I'm sure she shares all the details with her girlfriends—they're all bitches, too—and maybe they even—"

"Monsieur Tach, please!"

"This will teach you to record me, young man! If you took notes like any honest journalist, you could censor the senile horrors I'm sharing with you. With your machine, however, there is no way you can sort out my pearls from my filthy rubbish."

"And once the nurse has left?"

"She's left already? You don't waste time. Once she's left, it's already six o'clock or later. That bitch has gotten me in my pajamas, like a baby you bathe and wrap up in his rompers before giving him his last bottle. By then I feel so infantile that I play."

"You play? What do you play?"

"Anything. I drive around in my wheelchair, I set up a slalom, I play darts—look at the wall behind you, you'll see the damage—or else, supreme delight, I tear out the bad pages in classic novels."

"What?"

"Yes, I expurgate. *La Princesse de Clèves*, for example: it's an excellent novel, but it's far too long. I don't suppose you have read it, so I recommend the version I have taken the pains to abridge: a quintessential masterpiece."

"Monsieur Tach, what would you say if, three centuries from now, someone tore the pages deemed superfluous from your novels?"

"I challenge you to find even one superfluous page in my books."

"Madame de La Fayette would have told you the same thing."

"You're not going to compare me to that schoolgirl, are you?"

"Really, Monsieur Tach…"

"Would you like to know my secret dream? An auto-da-fé. A fine auto-da-fé of my entire work! That's shut you up, hasn't it?"

"Fine. And after your entertainment?"

"You are obsessed with food, I swear! The moment I talk about anything else, you get me onto the subject of food again."

"I am not obsessed, but since we started on that subject, we have to see it through to the end."

"You're not obsessed? You disappoint me, young man. So let's talk about food, since it doesn't obsess you. When I've finished expurgating, and have had a good round of darts, and slalomed and played nicely, when these educational activities have made me forget the horrors of my bath, I switch on the television, the way little children do, watching their idiotic programs before they have their Pablum or their alphabet soup. At that time of day, it's very interesting. There are endless commercials, primarily about food. I channel surf in order to put together the longest sequence of commercials on earth: With the sixteen European channels, it is perfectly feasible, if you surf intelligently, to get a full half-hour of uninterrupted commercials. It's a marvelous multilingual opera: Dutch shampoo, Italian cookies, German organic washing powder, French butter, and so on. What a treat. When the programs get too inane, I switch off the television. I've worked up an appetite after all the hundreds of commercials I've seen, so I set about making some food. You're pleased, aren't you? You should have seen your face, when I pretended to be getting off the subject again. Rest assured, you'll get your scoop. In the evening I have a fairly light meal. I'm perfectly happy with cold dishes, such as rillettes, solidified fat, raw bacon, the oil from a tin of sardines—I don't like the sardines very much, but they do flavor the oil, so I throw out the sardines and save the juice, and drink it on its own… Good heavens, what's wrong?"

"Nothing. Please continue."

"You don't look very well, I assure you. Along with that I heat up a very fatty bouillon, prepared ahead of time: For hours, I boil cheese rind, pig's trotters, chicken rumps, marrowbones, and a carrot. I add a ladleful of lard, remove the carrot, and let it cool for twenty-four hours. In fact, I like to drink the bouillon when it's cold, when the fat has hardened into a crust that leaves my lips glistening. But don't worry, I don't waste a thing, don't go thinking that I throw out all that delicate meat. After I've boiled it for a long time, the meat gains in unctuousness what it's lost in juice: The chicken rumps are a real treat, the yellow fat takes on a lovely spongy texture…What is the matter?"

"I… I don't know. Claustrophobia, perhaps. Could we open a window?"

"Open a window, on January 15? Don't even think about it. The oxygen would kill you. No, I know what you need."

"Please let me go out for a moment."

"It's out of the question, stay where it's warm. I'm going to make you one of my very own Brandy Alexanders, with melted butter."

Upon hearing this, the journalist's livid complexion turned bright green: He went off at a run, bent double, his hand on his mouth.

Tach wheeled at full tilt to the window overlooking the street, and had the intense satisfaction of contemplating the unfortunate man on his knees, retching, overwhelmed.

The fat man muttered into his four chins, jubilant, "When you have a delicate constitution, you don't go trying to measure up to Prétextat Tach!"

Hidden behind the net curtain, he could indulge in the delight of seeing without being seen, and he witnessed two men running out of the café across the street, to hurry over to their colleague who, his guts now empty, lay on the sidewalk next to his tape recorder, which he had not switched off: He had recorded the sound of his own vomiting.

The journalist had collapsed on the bench in the bistro and was recovering as best he could. He said again and again, his expression bleak, "No more food… I don't ever want to eat again…"

They got him to drink a little bit of lukewarm water that he eyed suspiciously. His colleagues wanted to listen to the tape; he intervened.

"Not in my presence, I beg you."

They called the victim's wife, and she came to collect him with her car. Once he had left, they could at last switch on the tape recorder. The writer's words aroused disgust, laughter, and enthusiasm.

"This guy is a gold mine. He's what I'd call a force of nature."

"He's wonderfully abject."

"At least he's someone who doesn't belong to soft ideology."

"Or lite ideology!"

"There's something about the way he throws his adversary."

"He's really good at it. I would not say as much for our friend. He fell into every trap."

"I don't like to speak badly about someone who's not here, but what was he thinking, asking him all those questions about food! I can see why the fat man wouldn't put up with it. When you have the opportunity to question such a genius, you don't go talking about food."

Deep inside, the journalists were delighted they had not had to go first or second. In the secrecy of their own good faith, they knew that if they had been in the shoes of their two unfortunate predecessors, they would have brought up the same subjects—stupid to be sure, but mandatory—and they were delighted that as a result they would not have to do the dirty work: They could put their best face forward, and make the most of it, although this did not prevent them from having a bit of a laugh at the expense of the victims.

So, on that terrible day when the entire world trembled at the prospect of imminent war, an adipose, paralytic, unarmed old man had managed to draw the attention of a handful of media priests away from the Persian Gulf. There was even one who, on that night when all were sleepless, went to bed on an empty stomach and slept the heavy, exhausting sleep of those who suffer from liver complaints, with nary a thought for those who were about to die.

Tach was milking the little known resources of disgust for all they were worth. Fat was his napalm, Brandy Alexanders were his chemical weapon.

That evening, he rubbed his hands together, a gleeful strategist.

FICTION

PROBABILIDAD

Eloy Urroz

Translated by Ezra E. Fitz

I'll begin by confessing that seeing the shape of Irene's ass—the perfection of that ass combined with the perfection of her body—was a determining factor, an incentive, but not the only one, for I don't want to give the impression that I focused solely there, because in my heart I didn't fixate on that part of her at all (those of you who know me know this). I would also incur accusations of blatant hypocrisy, I think, if I didn't admit some attraction to Irene's thick, luxuriant backside, which—I must add—is perhaps just a bit too large for her svelte, sculptured body. But what is one to do? That is her body and that is her ass and I've always been attracted to both, which is to say, the apparent or real disproportion, which is fundamentally a perfection, from a certain point of view. Her beautiful ass was the first thing that I saw as she walked into the conference hall, her hips swinging back and forth, always showing me her back (or her buttocks), but that alone would not have been enough. In fact, it was only when she turned around right in front of me, and I could finally see her round face and dark eyes, that I found myself struck, perplexed, and even a little bit scared. Actually, I was very scared. "But why?" you will ask. "Scared of what?" you will of course want to know. This is the hardest part to explain, but I will cut to the chase and not fall into the litany of digressions that have made so many contemporary novels and short stories unbearable to read, especially when I am forced to read them against my sovereign will. I was terrified because Irene, my current wife, looked identical (or almost identical) to the one person I love most in the world: my daughter Dulce, with the patent difference in age, of course. What I mean is that Irene could more or less be a perfect portrait of what I always imagined my young, sweet Dulce would look like as a young woman; that is, when she was twenty-four years old, twenty years after the day when I saw Irene for the first time at a conference organized by the Department of Romance Languages at the University of San Francisco, to which I was invited as the keynote speaker, to give a talk about Pancho Villa and how he was on the verge of perishing from being poisoned with very bad milk provided by a Japanese cook, an incident that very few historians are aware of, by the way.

It was in the midst of a formidable swing of the hips that Irene and I made eye contact, smiled to one another, and introduced ourselves; in fact, she took a long, expeditious look at the name tag hanging around my neck before telling me that I had the same name as her father, and that, of course, it was a very unusual name indeed: Eusebio, Eusebio, she murmured, barely pursing her beautiful crimson lips. But the chitchat was interrupted when we noticed that a conference session was about to begin, and all the other invited professors were returning to their seats in the lecture hall. She said it was a pleasure to meet me, and then she went away. It wasn't until later that afternoon that I approached her again and invited her out for a bite to eat. But the truly odd thing was that she replied with an absolute directness that she was not, in fact, hungry, but that she did want to go out because there was something truly quite important that she needed to tell me. "To discuss," actually, is what she said, leaving me astonished, since we hadn't even gotten to know each other yet, and already there was something we needed "to discuss," something quite specific, hence her need to advertise it in advance. Although I had specifically asked her out "to eat," she suggested we go out for drinks in the city, and that is how, at eight o'clock that night, we ended up in a lovely little restaurant by the bay on Fisherman's Wharf, where we ordered (again without coming to an agreement) a bowl brimming with exquisite clam chowder which we quickly dispatched along with a plate of fried calamari and a bottle of red Napa wine which I ordered myself.

It was during dinner that I began to realize, little by little, why Irene had agreed so readily to go out with me despite having a number of reasons for not doing such a thing. I'll list them here. First, the fact that I never removed my wedding ring; I either forgot about it, or perhaps it simply didn't matter to me, but then again, maybe I did so on purpose (although I very much doubt this latter explanation, as it isn't exactly my style of doing things, so I prefer either of the two former options, though I must admit I'm not certain about either of them). Second, Irene had a fiancée, a Gringo who loved her passionately and had received his PhD in literature from the same university as she. The third thing working against us (or, as I should humbly say, against me) was the fact that there was (and of course there still is) a twenty-year difference in our ages, as well as the fact that—whether it's nature or my own ancestors who are to blame—I am not what some would consider a particularly attractive man; however, it was precisely my physical appearance and the circumstances we found ourselves in which, in the end, prevailed against all the probabilities—or, as they say in English, "against all odds," which is much more linguistically precise than the Spanish term "probabilidad," which is ambiguous and can signify any one of a number of things—and I ended up with a beautiful, young, sexual woman like Irene, with an ass and a body as amazing as hers, who ordinarily would never have paid attention to an unattractive (though not incredibly ugly) married man twenty years her senior. But what aspect of my physical appearance have I confessed to, other than my mild ugliness? Nothing, save for what I've already mentioned, and the fact that I was—as Irene said, holding her glass of wine in a trembling hand—exactly like her father, even in age.

I was astonished by the revelation, so much so that I couldn't help but contemplate her there, sitting across the table from me, witnessing what I could swear was my daughter Dulce twenty years into the future, listening to her silky voice, looking into her eyes, observing Dulce's mouth and neck, and her hand gestures, because even then, and despite the twenty years between the two of them, the similarity was already quite astounding. I couldn't contain myself (though perhaps the wine had something to do with that) and so I showed her a picture of my little girl that I kept and still do keep in my wallet, and Irene—without so much as a word between the moment I showed her the photo and the moment she accepted it with her thin, tremulous fingers—was petrified... or nearly so. She dropped her almost empty glass, spilling a few drops of wine onto the tablecloth, and the first words out of her mouth were: "We're almost identical; I mean, she looks exactly like I did when I was her age." And then she opened her purse and took out a photo of a young girl, five or six years old, embracing a man of perhaps twenty-seven who was clearly her father and who (I must confess) looked extremely similar to me—at least, similar to me when I was that age, since I've grown a bit in the waistline, thanks to alcohol and the Wendy's hamburgers which I love, despite Irene's protests to the contrary.

But one other detail is missing, and perhaps it is more important than I led you to believe, when I mentioned it in passing, and that is the issue of our then-current circumstances. This doesn't have to do with the common things we've found in our life from time to time; rather, it's a very different thing, which I'll tell you about now: My lovely Irene had only recently (no more than a year before we met, I believe) lost her father, who of course was still a relatively young man at the time (my age, in fact, forty-three years old) in the most tragic circumstances you might imagine—in the strict sense of how I understand the term today, after having read the Greek legends—which is to say, it was the result of a bee sting, something which nobody, not even he himself, knew he was allergic to. It happened during a family vacation, and so his daughter was unfortunately present for everything, or almost everything, up to when he was admitted into the hospital. After that, the next time she saw her father, he was in a coffin. With tears welling up in her eyes, though she didn't let a single one fall, she told me that night at the restaurant in San Francisco: "And besides the name and the physical similarities, Eusebio, you have his sense of humor. How can I say it... it's in your gestures, your tics, everything. Strange, right? Don't you think?" And then I, impelled either by emotion or alcohol or the ardor between my legs, took her hand underneath the table and the wine-stained tablecloth and squeezed it, despite the fact that I knew full well that I hadn't yet had the opportunity to demonstrate my true sense of humor or any of my many tics (all of which are quite irritating, by the way). But what did my action imply? Solidarity? Compassion? Affection? Pity? Concern? Desire? Love? The urge to fuck? I suppose it was all of the above, a mixture of everything that my beloved Empedocles would simply consider Love.

However, for those who are paying attention, there is (or could be) an objection to the conclusion that my own life is the reason why I ended up teaching there, in the United States, married to Irene with a son, a second little sprout, as attractive and astute as his mother. And the objection is thus: if Dulce, my daughter, is as beautiful as I've said she is, and she doesn't even remotely resemble her father, which is to say, me, who is ugly or at least some-what so, then by default, she must resemble her mother, and if that were the case, then logically my first wife Fedra should look very similar to Irene, which simply isn't the case. If what I'm drawing up for you in a matter of sentences is really the case, then who the hell does my daughter look like? Quickly, I believe she looks most like her grandmother Dulce: my handsome ex-mother-in-law who at some providential moment was willing to take care of her granddaugh-ter Dulce but didn't end up doing so on account of me, who chose to run off to a conference in San Francisco all by myself, which resulted in the subsequent ups-and-downs of this particular case.

To the aforementioned (and patently evident) objection, I'd like to add another one, dear Reader: the fact that if Eusebio, Irene's father, looked so much like me, and therefore wasn't very handsome, then Irene should look rather like her mother, something which (I knew at once) also wasn't the case. So the only solution to this part of the riddle is that Irene had, in fact, been adopted by Cuban-American parents, and that she (I would later learn) had actually been born in Mexico.

After that encounter on Fisherman's Wharf, which was followed by a long stroll along the bay, things continued to happen, one after another, leading (inevitably, of course) to my separation from Fedra, the supremely difficult deci-sion to leave my daughter Dulce (not my mother-in-law Dulce) and eventually to my marriage to Irene in San Francisco: a strange substitution (I know) of a young girl for a young woman, because even today, when I return home after spending three hours in one of those abominable academic committees, I am always amazed to see the incredible similarities between the two of them… and that, of course, results (for better or for worse) in bringing back many memories of the two of us together, my daughter and I chasing each other down the hallway of our house in Coyoacán, playing hide-and-seek among the rattan furniture, spending hours sprawled out on the spongy carpet putting together a Sleeping Beauty puzzle, wrestling and horsing around, listening to songs by Cri Cri the singing cricket, going hand-in-hand for ice cream at Siberia, buying a globe at the plaza and smothering her with kisses, perfectly happy with the heavenly gift which today seems so very far away from me.

FREE VERSES TO MY SON

Natalia Sannikova

Translated by Matvei Yankelevich

When you've read as many books, poems, and blogs
as I've already read,
you'll find out just how little I get literature.
For example, Blok—he wrote about Woman and the Revolution,
a worthy endeavor for a poet.
Yesenin drank, loved, made trouble, and died young—
that too, all things considered, is typical.
Brodsky was in exile and in Venice, ended up on the Nobel list—
nothing odd about that fate, especially in our times.
Poets in my circle, who your children will study in Russian Lit.,
every day write wonderful things in online journals—
essays, poems, fresh thoughts on politics and literature.
Outside the windows it's winter again, I think about you, and I think
how summer will come, for the first time without happiness in it for me.
Please don't read anything at all, save for books on programming.
I don't want you to figure it all out about me—
about just how little I get life.
And love—but that you definitely won't figure out.

Natalia Sannikova participated in the 2010 PEN World Voices Festival.

FICTION

ADMIRATION

Quim Monzó

Translated by Mary Ann Newman

The girl listens in amazement as the cryptic novelist reads a chapter of his latest novel. When he finishes, everyone applauds. She manages to maneuver herself into a strategic position and, as the novelist leaves the room, chatting with this one and that, shaking the occasional hand, she approaches him. She tells him she's very interested in his work and, if possible, she'd like to get to know him in depth. The girl is pretty and the novelist likes pretty girls. When he looks at her, she meets his gaze and smiles. The novelist agrees. He brushes off the organizers and they go to a restaurant for dinner.

It's a no-frills restaurant because, even though he's a very good novelist (or precisely because he is), he doesn't do well enough financially to afford expensive restaurants. This doesn't matter at all to her. She's fallen (she realizes it as she looks into his eyes) totally and completely in love. He talks and talks without stopping, and she likes what he says. She laughs a lot and they leave the restaurant with their arms around each other. They go to his place, on a top floor with no elevator (she waxes enthusiastically, "Just like in the movies!") where they spend the night. They see each other again the following day.

They end up living together. Four months later, she gets pregnant. They have a boy. The apartment becomes not only too small, but much too uncomfortable for rearing a child. One evening the cryptic novelist makes a decision; one way or another, he has to bring in more money. Cryptic novels hardly make a penny. And what they earn between the two of them from his chess columns for the newspaper and her work as a clerk in a cosmetics shop is peanuts.

Fortunately, a friend of his (who published a couple of books of poetry some years before and now produces TV commercials) finds him a job in an advertising agency. He starts off as a copywriter. He's never been short of wit and he certainly knows how to write. So much so that the managers soon realize

Quim Monzó participated in the 2010 PEN World Voices Festival.

his worth. Things start to improve, both economically and professionally.

Finally they can move. She gets pregnant again. Occasionally he recalls the days when he wrote cryptic novels. Those days grow more and more distant. It's a closed chapter, and at times it even seems impossible that he had ever devoted himself to cryptic novels. He wouldn't go back to it for anything in the world. Literature seems like something moth-eaten to him now, an art of centuries past. The future, the present, is not in books, which no one reads anymore, but in newspapers, television, the radio. And advertising is the highest art in this arena, because it prostitutes itself consciously. And so it is that three years later he has his own agency. He comes home every day totally worn out, with just enough time to give his two daughters a kiss before he stretches out on the sofa with a loud sigh and tells his wife at machine-gun speed the thousand events of the day.

The woman looks at him pityingly. She knows he doesn't miss the days in which he wrote cryptic novels. She knows that he struggles each day from sunrise to sunset for the good of their household, and that he does it gladly, and that, what's more, he's been successful at it, and this makes him happy. Most likely he would not understand her pitying him, but she does. And so when he goes to bed and falls right to sleep, she leaves her light on, reading a novel. It's an intricate novel (the new rage—cryptic novels are no longer in fashion) that came out just two weeks before and in those two weeks has become a success, a tremendous success in what's left of the world of literature. She finds it exhilarating, so much so that she has no intention of missing the reading the novelist will be giving the following afternoon at a prestigious cultural center in the city.

ONE WAY TO DISAPPEAR

Lilli Carré

My sister and I lived in a house near Dorado Park.

They'd spin them around and leave them disoriented in the grass.

The park is unusually large and all the trees look alike, so the people who are let loose there end up walking the grassy plains while growing old and looking for a road or a building.

Sis and I watched those people bumble about while we ran a joke writing business from home.

It was because of the guy
she met at the bus stop.

She brought him in from the rain, and he took
to her like an overly-affectionate cat
that wouldn't leave her lap.

The more time they spent in each other's company, the wilder they became. They soon spoke an invented language and lived by a new sort of logic.

I eventually stopped writing them, and we all resorted to eating the fruit that grew from my sister's wildness in order to sustain ourselves.

The house became overgrown,
and Sis disappeared into her own thicket,
along with the guy from the bus stop.

Now the house was boring but dangerous. All I really did was watch people get spun around to wander the park forever, while fighting off what Sis had left behind.

A stray beast bit my leg and I decided it was useless to stay there, so I slid out the window because I couldn't find the door.

I took a few steps into Dorado Park
and noticed that all the trees looked the same.

FICTION

THE PRETTY GROWN-TOGETHER CHILDREN

Megan Mayhew Bergman

Let me tell it, I said.

No, you're a liar and a drunk, I said. Or she said.

Our voices could be like one. I could feel hers in my bones, especially when she sang—a strong quicksilver soprano.

One of us has to tell it, I said, and it's going to be me.

An agent had come to see us. Or that's what he said he was. A talent scout. I couldn't remember his name. He wore a blue sports coat with heavy gold buttons, jeans, loafers. His hair shone with tonic, and he knew how to shake hands. My bones ached from his grip.

Look, I said to Violet. I'm a better storyteller. You sing, I tell stories.

Violet didn't answer. She had vanished, the way the great Harry Houdini had taught us to do in the RKO cafeteria. When you're tired of each other, he had said, imagine retreating into an imaginary shell. A giant conch. Harry was short and bowlegged. Parted down the middle, his curly hair splayed across his forehead into a heart shape. Separate *mentally*, he had said.

What about when Billie is indiscreet? With men? Violet had asked. What do I do then?

Same thing you've done in the past, I had said. Look away.

Violet was like that. Made her voice rise when she wanted to play innocent. She pretended to be shy. But I could feel her blood get warm when she spoke to men she admired. I could feel her pulse quicken.

Back in the RKO cafeteria days we had floor-length raccoon coats, matching luggage, tortoise-shell combs and soft lipstick. We had money in the bank. We took cabs in the city. We traveled, kissed famous men. We had been on film. The '30s, '40s, even the '50s. Those had been our decades. We had thrived.

In the RKO days, people thought our bodies were the work of God.

But now we were two old show girls bagging groceries at the Sack and Save in Aberdeen. There were no more husbands, no boyfriends. Just fat women and their dirty-nosed children pointing fingers in the grocery line.

Can y'all help us get these bags out to the car, they'd ask.

I'd never met so many mean-hearted women in my life. Violet and I were still able-bodied, but we were old. Our knuckles hurt from loading bags. Our knees swelled from all the standing. But we'd do it to keep our boss happy, hauling paper bags to station wagons in the parking lot.

I jes want to see it walk, the kids would whisper.

We lived in a singlewide trailer with a double bed and a hot plate the grocer had let us have behind his house. Mice ran through the walls, ate holes through our cereal boxes.

Look, the agent said. I'm going to come back tomorrow and we're going to talk about some projects I have in mind.

Come after supper, I said.

Houdini had told us: Never appear eager to be famous.

The agent came closer. His cologne was fresh. He made Violet nervous, but not me. He reached for each of our hands and kissed our knuckles.

Until then, he said, and disappeared through the screen door. The distinctive sound of the summer night rushed inside. Cicadas, dry leaves rattling in the woods, a single car on the dirt road.

Some nights Violet and I sat on the cinderblock steps outside, rubbing our bare toes in the cool dirt, painting our nails. Like most twins, we didn't have to talk. We were somewhere between singular and plural.

After the agent left, Violet and I sat on an old velour couch, turning slightly away from each other as our bodies mandated. I forgot how long we'd been sitting there. There were framed pictures of people we didn't know on the walls. The kitchen table had three legs. One had been chewed and hovered over the linoleum like a bum foot. The curtains smelled like tobacco. The radio was tuned to a stock car race.

Rex White takes second consecutive pole.

Violet was still, hands on her knees. She was probably thinking about an old boyfriend she had once. Ed. Violet had really loved Ed. He was a boxer with a mangled face and strange ears that I didn't care for. He wasn't fit for a star, I told her. When she went into her shell I figured that's who she went there with.

I was hot and dizzy. Our trailer had no air conditioning.

Post-menopausal, I figured. I needed water.

I stood up.

Violet came out of her imaginary shell.

We have to get some money, she said, as we moved toward the sink. We have to get out of here. I have paper cuts from the grocery bags. My ankles are swollen. How come you never want to sit down?

I'm working on it, I said. Besides, we're professionals. We've got something left to offer the world.

I let the faucet sputter until the water ran clear.

One of us could die, I said. And they'd have to cut the other loose.

So that's what it takes, Violet said, and disappeared into herself again.

I was told our mother was disgusted when she tried to breastfeed us.

Just a limp tangle of arms and legs. Too many heads to keep happy, Miss Hadley said. Lips everywhere. Strange cries.

Miss Hadley, our mother's midwife, was our first guardian. We lived with her in a ramshackle house that was part yellow, part white—the eyesore house on the nice side of town. The magnolia trees were overgrown and scratched the windows. The screened-in porch was packed with magazines, rusted bikes, broken lamps, boxes of old clothes and library books.

Weren't for me you'd be dead, Miss Hadley said. I found a wet nurse. I *saved* you.

Like stacks of coupons, bread cartons, magazines—we were one of the things Miss Hadley collected, lined her nest with.

Once, when you was toddlers, you got out the door nekkid and upset the neighborhood, she said. She liked to remind us, or maybe herself, of her generosity. Her ability to *tolerate*.

Carolina-born, Miss Hadley looked like she was a hundred years old. Her cheeks sank downward. She had a fleshy chin and a mouthful of bad teeth.

Billie, she'd say, I'm fixin' to get after you.

And she would. She once threw a raw potato at my forehead when she found me rummaging in the pantry after dinner. Miss Hadley slapped my knees and arms with the flyswatter when I talked back. Sometimes she'd get Violet by accident.

She ain't do nothing to you, I'd say. Leave her be.

Don't sass me, she'd say. You've got the awfullest mouth for a girl your age.

When we were young, Violet and I had the thickest bangs you'd ever seen, enormous bows in our hair. There were velvet ribbons around our waist, lace dresses, music lessons. We were almost pretty.

We learned how to smile graciously, how to bask in the charity of the Christian women in the neighborhood. We learned to use the toilet at the same time. We helped each other with homework and chores.

Miss Hadley kept a dirty house, scummy dishes in the sink. There was hair on the floor, toilets that didn't work, litters of rescued dogs that commanded the couch. Her stained glass windows were cracked. The front door was drafty. Entire rooms were filled with magazines. Her husband was dead (if she'd ever really had one) and she had no children except for us. And looking back, we weren't her children at all. We were a business venture.

We fired the shotgun at Beaufort's Terrapin Races, presented first place ribbons at hog and collard festivals. We crowned Wilson's Tobacco Queens, opened for the Bluegrass Boys at various music halls. We knew high-stepping cloggers, competitive eaters, the local strong men. We knew showmanship.

I remember my line from the Terrapin Races: *And now, ladies and gentlemen, the tortoise race.* Years later, when I woke up in the middle of the night in a hot flash, that line would come to me.

We didn't know to be unhappy. We didn't know we were getting robbed blind. We didn't know about all the money we'd made for Miss Hadley.

I don't charge you rent, she said at the dinner table. But I should charge for those hungry mouths.

We believed ourselves to be in her debt. We were *grateful*, even.

Miss Hadley's yard was overgrown with ivy, honeysuckle, and scuppernong vines. When we hated what she'd made for dinner—she was a terrible cook— we'd go out hunting scuppernongs, eat them fresh off the vine. I liked them best when they looked like small potatoes, soft, golden, and dusty. I had to tug Violet out the front door to eat them. If we came in smelling of fruit, Miss Hadley would come after us with the switches.

Ya'll been eating scuppanons again, she'd say, catching the back of our legs. Scuppydines is for poor kids.

We lived in what had been the maid's room, behind the kitchen. We shared a double bed, slept back-to-back. There was a poster of President Hoover tacked to the wall. Violet papered our drawers with sheet music and hid licorice in her underwear. Miss Hadley had lined the room in carpet samples. I kept a cracker tin full of movie stubs and magazines.

Violet and I lay in bed at night talking about the latest sheet music, or a boy who had come with his parents to see us play at the music hall. We talked about lace socks, travelling to Spain, how we'd one day hear ourselves on the radio, learn to dance beautifully with a partner on each side.

I want to waltz, Violet said.

I want a new dress first, I said. Or to sing "April in Paris" on the radio.

Teaching you to walk was some ugly business, Miss Hadley often said. Dancing—I can only imagine. You girls need to work at sitting still, staying pretty. That's why you've learned to read music.

Violet and I—we had thick skin.

We slept with an army of rescued greyhounds, lithe and flea-bitten, in our bed at night. We fed them dinner rolls, put our fingers on their dull teeth, let them keep us warm.

There were no secrets. Imagine: You could say nothing, do nothing, eat nothing, touch nothing, love nothing without the other knowing.

Like King Tut's death mask, we were exhibited.

The calling card, as I remember it: "If we have interested you, kindly tell your friends to come visit us." *The Pretty Grown-Together Children.*

There were stacks of these in Miss Hadley's basement, smeared across the kitchen table. Stacks in every grocery store and Laundromat in town.

Hear the twins sing "Dream a Little Dream of Me." Hear the twins recite Lord Byron's "Fare Thee Well."

Miss Hadley sat us on a piano bench or leather trunk to play our instruments. We crossed our legs at the ankles. She set out a blue glass vase which she instructed visitors to deposit money into.

I took these girls in out of the goodness of my heart, she'd say, and I'd appreciate you donating from the goodness of yours so that they can continue their music lessons.

Bless your hearts, the ladies would say, coming up close to inspect us.

Children would ask: Does it hurt? Do you fight? You think about cutting that skin yourself?

It did not hurt to be joined—we knew no difference. As for fighting, yes, but we were masters of compromise: *I'll read books now if you'll go walking later. You pick the movie this week and I'll pick next. We can get in bed but I'm going to keep the lamp on so I can read. We can sleep in but you owe me a dollar.*

At night, our legs intertwined. This was not like touching someone else's leg. It wasn't like touching my own, either. It was comforting, warm. We were, despite our minds' best efforts, one body.

You kick, Violet told me. You dream violent dreams.

Your arms twitch, I said, though it wasn't true.

After Miss Hadley's death, when the movers began emptying her house, our fliers were used to protect the dishes. We were wadded up and stuffed into teacups. Our advertisements scattered across her dry yard. Scuppernongs lay bird-picked and smashed on the lawn. The greyhounds were leashed to the front porch. I remember you could see the sun shining through the translucent skin on their heels. I remember thinking—what now?

When Miss Hadley got the fever we were willed to her cousin Samson like a house. I'm afraid to tell you about the kind of man he was, how our skin got thicker. I'll tell you this. His house was dark, unpainted, and smelled of pipe smoke. Samson did not shower or shave. He didn't parade us in public or charge to hear us play music. In fact, the music lessons stopped. He kept us inside. He had other interests. I won't say more.

C'mere sweetmeats, he used to say, patting his lap.

Ya'lls never been loved properly, he'd say.

There were months when we did not leave the house other than for school and church. It occurred to us to be depressed about our situation, scared. This was the first time we had been truly unhappy.

We were sixteen. One night we packed a bag of our best clothes, my saxophone, her clarinet. We waited until Samson was good and drunk, then left out the back door and caught a bus to New York. We'd never moved so fast together, never been so in sync.

The bag is heavy, Violet said. And my feet hurt in these pumps.

It's worth every blister, I said. Trust me.

Each step I thought of his breath. His fingers. The pain went away.

We made it to the station, sweating in our high heels with turned ankles and empty stomachs.

Violet and I swore, in the back seat of that bus to New York, that we'd never mention Samson again. We'd pretend the things he'd done had never happened. The bruises on our thighs would heal and the patches of our hair would grow back. Until then we'd wear hats. We'd practice music on our own. We'd get back into the business.

When we couldn't pay the bus driver, he dropped us off at the police station. We were freezing. We'd never had a jacket made to fit us.

Put on your lipstick, I said to Violet.

I still like to think of that dimestore lipstick. It was soft and crimson and made me feel beautiful.

Excuse me, I said to a man smoking a cigarette on the cement steps.

He looked up at us in disbelief. He wore a three-piece suit and a tweed cap. His lips were full and it hurt me to watch him sink his front teeth into his bottom lip.

I could see my breath in the air. The sound of New York was different than the sound of Miss Hadley's back yard. The street looked wet; there were bricks everywhere, lights lining the sidewalks. We were petrified. I could feel Violet's blood pressure rising.

I never seen something so pretty and so strange, he said.

And that's how we got hooked up with Martin Lambert.

The agent will be back tomorrow, I said to Violet.

I can't read this if you're going to keep pacing that way, she said, trying to get through an old copy of *Reader's Digest* while I bustled about the bedroom.

Our bed in the grocer's trailer had one set of threadbare sheets and a pale pink quilt. I picked at the frayed edges when I couldn't sleep.

Are you eating another cookie? I asked.

Old stock, Violet said, crumbs on her mouth. Someone has to eat them. Grocer was going to throw them out.

Our cupboard was stocked with dented soup cans and out-of-date beans. The grocer let us take a bag of old food home at the end of each week.

I noticed the lines around Violet's eyes. I guessed they were around mine too. Our skin was getting thinner, our bones fragile. Our fingers bled at work.

Help me get this suitcase on the bed, I said.

Violet used one hand to help.

Between us we had one brown leather suitcase full of custom clothes. There were dresses, bathing suits, pants, and nightgowns. Those we'd had for decades were moth-eaten and thin.

We've gotta mend these, I said. And not get fat.

No one's looking, she said, her mouth full of stale oatmeal cookie.

The agent is looking, I said.

This wasn't the first time Violet had tried to sabotage our success. Once, she'd dyed her hair blonde. Then she tried to get fat. Every time I turned around in the '40s she was eating red velvet cupcakes.

Your teeth are gonna go blood red from all that food coloring, I said.

We had enough strikes against us in the looks department. One of Violet's eyes sloped downward, as if it might slide off her face. I hated that eye. I felt like we could have been more without it. Like Virginia Mayo or Eve Arden or someone with a good wardrobe and a contract or two.

Give me the cookies, I said.

No one's looking, she said. I told you.

The agent is looking, I said again. We can't show up naked. We can't show up in grocery aprons.

Violet held the cookie box in her right arm. I could let her have it, tackle her, or run in a circle. I was too tired for the game. We'd played it enough as kids.

Fine, I said. Eat your damn cookies.

We each had talents. Violet could disappear inside her imaginary shell. I could go without food for days. Martin Lambert had intended to take us to his sister's house that first night in New York.

I can't have you home with me, he said. We'll figure something out.

He flagged down a cab.

I can't feel my feet, Violet whispered.

I wasn't sure we'd ever been up so late before. The lights of the Brooklyn Bridge pooled in the East River. The people on the sidewalks wore beautiful jackets. Soldiers were home with girls on their arms, cigarettes on their lips. Restaurants kept their lights on past midnight.

I hoped Violet wouldn't tell him it was our first cab ride. The stale smell of tobacco oozed from the upholstery. Martin lit another cigarette and rubbed his palms on his pants. He kept looking at us out of the corner of his eye. Staring without staring. Disbelief. Curiosity.

I wanted to be close to him. I wanted to smell his aftershave, touch the hair under his cap.

We sing, I said. We can swim and roller skate. Violet plays clarinet, I play saxophone.

Well I'll be, he said. Showbiz twins. Working gals.

Martin shook his head and chewed his lip. One thing I'd learned—people saw different things when they looked at us. Some saw freaks, some saw love. Some saw opportunity.

Violet was quiet.

We want to be in the movies, I said.

How old are you? he asked.

Eighteen, I said.

I pulled the hem of my dress above my knees.

Violet jabbed me in the ribs.

Honest, I said.

Violet placed a hand over her mouth and giggled.

Cabbie, Martin said. Stop at McHale's. Looks like we're going to grab ourselves a few drinks.

Our hats were out of style and out of season, but we were used to standing out in a crowd.

Martin rushed over to a stocky man standing by the bar.

Ed, he said. I want you to meet Billie and Violet.

Ed nodded but didn't speak. The two men turned to lean over their beers and speak quietly.

I felt a hundred eyes burning my back.

Look at the bodies, not the faces, I told myself.

Miss Hadley had said: Learn to love the attention. You don't have a choice.

There is no one in the world like you, I said to myself.

The imaginary spotlight is on, Violet said.

There is no one in the world like you.

We should find a hotel, Violet said. Then go south tomorrow. If we leave early, we could get to Richmond. Even Atlanta. Somewhere *nice*.

With what money? I asked her.

One gin and tonic later I pulled Violet onto the stage. The band was warming up. We could be seen and gawked at, or we could be appreciated, marveled over. I knew which I preferred.

The first night Martin and I slept together, Violet said the Lord's Prayer eighteen times.

...hallowed be thy name. Thy kingdom come, thy will be done...

Violet!

On Earth as it is in Heaven.

Just keep going, I said.

Are you sure? Martin asked.

Violet had one hand over her eyes, a half-hearted attempt not to watch. She kept her clothes on, even her shoes.

Yes, I told him.

The room was dark but Martin kept his eyes closed. He never kissed me on my mouth. Not then, not ever.

During the day, Violet and I worked the industrial mixer at a bakery. We shaped baguettes in the afternoons. Nights, we sang at McHale's. I began drinking. Ed and Martin sipped scotch at a corner table, escorted us back to our efficiency in the thin morning light.

We primped for our performances like starlets. In the shower, we rotated in and out of the water. Lather, turn, rinse, repeat.

Let's go for a natural look tonight, Violet said, sitting down at the second-hand bureau we'd turned into our vanity table.

I was thinking Jezebel, I said. Red lipstick and eyes like Elizabeth Taylor.

It looks better when we coordinate, Violet said.

I painted a thick, black line across my eyelid.

Let me do yours, I said, turning to her.

Some nights I felt like a woman—the warm stage lights on my face, the right kind of lipstick on, the sound of my voice filling the room, Violet singing harmony. Some nights I felt like two women. Some nights I felt like a two-headed monster. That's what some drunk had shouted as Violet and I took the stage. Ed had come out from behind his table swinging.

We were the kind of women that started fights. Not the kind of women that launched ships.

It took one year and one bottle of Johnnie Walker for Ed to confess his love for my sister.

Can you, um, read a newspaper or look away? he asked me.

I folded the newspaper to the crossword puzzle and chewed a pencil.

I been thinking, Ed said. You are a kind woman. A good woman.

Violet touched his cheek.

Does anyone know a four letter word for Great Lake? I asked.

I watch you sing every night, and every night I decide that one day I'm going to kiss you, he said.

Violet cupped the back of his neck with her hands.

Erie, I said. The word is Erie.

An hour later and they had moved to the bed. I watched the clock on the wall, recited Byron in my head.

Ed cried afterwards, laid his mangled face on Violet's chest.

I cried too.

When the agent comes, I said to Violet, let me do the talking.

We were taking a sponge bath in front of the kitchen sink, naked as blue jays. It was too hard getting in and out of a shower these days.

A cicada hummed somewhere in the windowsill.

Do you need more soap? Violet asked.

This is my plan to get out of here, I said. We'll offer him the rights to our life story. We can get by on a few thousand.

I dipped my washcloth into the cool water and held it between my breasts.

Violet touched the skin between us.

We'll be okay, she said. I don't want you to worry.

Martin had never stayed the night. He had a wife. I wondered what she was like, what she'd think of the things we did.

Normal people don't do the things you do in bed, Violet said.

Since when are we normal? I asked.

You could keep your eyes closed more, I said.

And my ears, Violet said, blushing.

Martin is a man's man, I told her. He knew what he wanted.

He was rough, sometimes clutching my neck or grabbing my hair. Afterwards he'd talk about the movies we'd get into, how he'd be our agent.

Like *The Philadelphia Story*, he said, but instead of Hepburn, there's Billie and Violet. Then he'd wash his hands, rinse his mouth, wet his hair down, and leave.

One month my period was late.

Jesusfuckingchrist is all Martin would say.

In bed at night I asked myself what I would do with a baby. What Violet and I would do. I convinced myself we could handle it. We had many hands.

Ed slept over those days. I watched Violet stroke his hair, trace the shape of his strange ears with her fingertip. She slept soundly on his chest.

One night Martin dragged us to an empty apartment around the corner from McHale's.

Stay here, he said, backing out of the door.

A man came in—my body aches when I think of it. He opened a bag of surgical instruments, spread a mat onto the floor.

Lie down, he said. Put your legs up like this.

I wanted to do right by Violet, keep Martin happy.

There was blood. Violet fainted. I no longer felt human. I felt as if I could climb out of my body.

We're done here, the man said. You shouldn't have this problem again.

We didn't leave our bed for weeks.

Martin disappeared.

He found the straight and narrow, Ed said. That operation of yours cost him two months' salary. He's somewhere in Cleveland now.

Ed brought us soup and old bread from the bakery while I recovered.

He continued to drink at the corner table nights when Violet and I sang. He was anxious, protective.

One night, after we'd performed "Tennessee Waltz," the bartender waved me over.

We've got leftover cake, Billie-girl, he said, pouring me a gin and tonic.

I ate half a sheet cake between songs.

Billie, Violet said. That's disgusting.

I pushed my empty glass forward for a refill.

The great Houdini told us to retreat to an imaginary shell when we got tired of the other one, I said to the bartender, rolling my eyes at Violet.

We never met Houdini, Violet said.

Next thing I knew, Violet was wrestling my finger out of my mouth in the bathroom stall.

Stop it! she said.

You drink too much and you never eat. What did you have yesterday? Half a peanut-butter sandwich? An apple?

We sank back against the wall of the bathroom stall. I still remember the pattern of the tile. Mint colored rectangles with black squares. Ice cream, I thought. Tiles like ice cream.

And the lying, Billie, she said. The lying.

I watched ankles and shoes walk by the bathroom stall. Some women had beautiful ankles. Some women moved on two feet instead of four.

I still had icing on my fingers.

I need to stay here for a while, I said.

Violet held her hand underneath the stall door and asked a pair of ankles for a glass of water.

She had chutzpah when I least expected it.

Two weeks later, she surprised us all by dropping her panties into the church time capsule.

Did I ever tell you about our big break? I asked the agent.

I pulled out a stock photo Violet and I had autographed.

It felt strange to offer an autograph now. Autographs were from important people. Violet and I might be broke and strange but we were not ordinary.

Why do you have that old thing out? Violet asked. What are we—seven or eight?

She was eating Saltines out of a dented tin box.

Can't whistle now, she said, smiling.

I pinched her bottom.

The agent is here, I whispered.

I'd once seen Violet cover my half of the photo with her hand to see what she looked like alone. We'd both wondered.

Here's how we ended up in Carolina. I'd been in talks with a man who said he needed us for some public relations work.

It's like this, he had said. You show up at the theater and do an introduction for my movie.

We have to take the risk, I'd said to Violet.

But we don't, she'd said. We're old. We're retired.

We can't live on what we have, I'd said. Not for long, and I plan on living a long time.

We fronted him money for travel arrangements. He promised a hefty return. But what he did was leave us stranded at the bus station. We had no money, no car, only our suitcase.

I'm tired of trusting, Violet said.

We cried that night, propped up against the brick station. A minister took us in, fed us hot dogs, said he knew of a local grocery that needed an extra pair of hands.

We have those, I said.

One night Violet shook me awake. Get up, she said, switching on the bedside lamp. Get up.

Your eye, I said.

Violet had a red handprint across her face.

Ed was in the bathroom with the door closed.

We stumbled to the dark kitchen.

He's drunk, she said.

Doesn't matter, I said.

I picked up the silver pot we used to boil noodles in one hand, grabbed a paring knife in the other.

Ed came into the kitchen crying.

Get out, I said.

I shielded Violet with my body, backed her up to the sink.

I flipped on the kitchen light. We all winced.

Leave, I said.

You're crazy, he said, sinking to his knees. Violet?

He'd said something else. What was it that he said?

I slung the silver pot into his crooked nose.

I can't picture what the agent looks like, I said to Violet.

Violet was reading jokes in *Reader's Digest* and eating outdated yogurt.

There was the one in Texas, I said. And then the one in the city. The one with the Buick.

We're in Carolina now, she said. Why don't you rest?

When the agent comes back, we should do a number, I said.

There hasn't been an agent here, Violet said. You have a fever.

Or I said. One of us was always saying things.

The one in the blue sport coat, I said. With gold buttons.

Do we have health insurance? she asked, the cool back of her hand against my forehead.

When the agent comes back, I said, let's do "April in Paris."

Let me get you a cool washcloth, she said, lifting me from the couch.

Let the water run clear, I said. Tomorrow…

Trust God on this one, Violet said. Rest.

In our early days, people had trusted God's intent. We were the way we were because He made it so.

I remembered what Ed had said to me that night I crushed his face. His mangled, fighter's face.

You are not made in His image, he'd said. You can't be.

And now, ladies and gentleman, the tortoise race.

My eyes watered. I felt as though I could no longer stand.

I jes want to see it walk.

I'm sorry, I said to Violet, before I pulled her to the ground.

If we have interested you, kindly tell your friends to come visit us.

There was something about the body, our seam…

I touched the skin between us.

One day soon, I said, you'll walk out of here alone.

Hush, Violet said. Hush.

Get a new dress, I said. Eat all the goddamn cookies you want.

THE BUG THAT ATE THE VEGETABLE

Akinwumi Isola

Translated by Akinloyé A. Òjó

I spoke endlessly, you refused totally,
I articulated incessantly, you kept shrugging your shoulders
I spoke it in codes, I spoke French,
You turned a deaf ear, you did not take it seriously.
You said I am overdoing it, that I am pestering you a lot.
Where exactly is my error?
Is it really my fault?
The bug that ate the vegetable isn't guilty,
There is a limit to a plant's beauty.
Whoever pursues Àsùnlé is guiltless.
Isn't there a limit to how beautiful a maiden can be!
Before you came, I had rejected others,
Before I met you, I had rebuffed the pleas of many,
I said I will be like the bat on a palm,
That hangs upside down, watching the acts of other birds.
Once bitten, twice shy
I said before I look at the face of another maiden,
It will be a while, it will be some time.
Hùn! the snail closed its door,
It says it will not answer the rain,
It is only the first rain of the year that has just fallen,
That has the snail carrying its house.
Wandering around the water with its horns,
It was peacefully by myself that I went to Gbági market

Akinloyé A. Òjó's translations of Akinwumi Isola were supported in part by the PEN Translation Fund.

I got to the front of Sánráì and I committed a grave offense
I saw the-light-skinned-beauty with gorgeous shoulders
I saw the-beautiful-eyed-one-that-wore-everything-fittingly
The black crown on Àsùnlé's head was fitting
It was more fitting than a prince's crown.
My heart beat faster as if I should cry,
My heart panted as if I should start my message
I again remembered my promise and kept quiet,
I kept quiet; I went on like a dummy.
Alas! Once the arrow of love strikes, it cannot be pulled out.
It is swiftly that strong alcohol intoxicates,
It is quickly that a child returns from discarded farms
I glanced back once, I glanced back again,
They implored Orò not to throw stones,
He says how about the one that he is holding?
My snail is attached to your tree.
The two faces of the dùndún drum only produce one tune.
Both you and I, our hearts have become one.
If the elephant likes, let it go into the forest
If the buffalo likes, let it return to the grassland,
If the bàtá drum goes on a journey
Let its ornament bells follow it.
Once I see you,
Whoever wants to go can leave.

DON'T SNATCH ÀBÈNÍ

Akinwumi Isola

Translated by Akinloyé A. Òjó

I cannot handle farming,
I am lazy,
I cannot hunt small game,
My wife has matured,
I do not have money!
The owner of twenty slaves must not take her,
The master of thirty servants must not snatch her.
Don't snatch Àbèní,
Don't snatch my woman.
He that snatches the wife of the lazy man snatches trouble,
If it were the rich man's wife,
He could marry another instead.
It is the stirring about that kills the pestle
I will recount the story in Adó
I will recount the story in Ede
I will report in Ìgbàrà Òkè
I will report up to Ìbàdàn.
Àbèní does not want money,
Àbèní does not want clothes:
The words of my mouth are soothing to Àbèní
The mouth of the wealthy cannot be as soothing.
I-the-one-with-honeysweet-voice,
The-smooth-sieving-lips.
I, the one that speaks to thrill the young,
The-thought-provoking-speaker for the old.
I have recited poetry in small settlements
I recited in the land of Aké

I recited in Ìbàdàn
As an indigene.
Olúbàdàn actually came to watch me.
I recited in Lagos,
They couldn't make fun of me.
I recited poetry for the landlords,
They gave me a house to live in,
I recited poetry for the owners of the path,
They bequeathed me with the road.
It is poetry that I recited.
They said that I wanted to snatch their woman.
We have wife,
We have wife.
It is poetry that you heard and you adjusted your headgear!
Àbèní is enough for me.
If it is a rich man that wants to snatch Àbèní,
He will fritter away his money,
If it is a chief that wants to snatch Àbèní,
He will use his crown as collateral for a debt,
The priest that wants to snatch Àbèní,
He will become an adversary of God,
It is me, Àjàní, that says so,
I am not saying this timorously.
Words will not tear my lips,
I have been saying this for a long time!

ENDLESS ARRIVAL

ADAM GOPNIK: I am a peculiar kind of émigré—a Canadian émigré. Some Canadian émigrés, when they come to America, regard their immigration as from a First World country to a Third World country. Let me read something that I wrote in my book *Through the Children's Gate* about seeing New York for the first time, when my parents brought me here for the opening of the Guggenheim Museum many years ago:

> For the Guggenheim occasion, my mother had sewn a suit of mustard-colored velvet for me and a matching dress for my sister, and we stood in line outside the corkscrew building, trying to remember what we had been taught about Calder. Afterward, we marched down the ramp of the amazing museum and then walked along Fifth Avenue, where we saw a Rolls-Royce. We ate dinner at a restaurant that served a thrilling, exotic mix of blintzes and insults, and that night we slept in my great-aunt Hannah's apartment at Riverside Drive and 115th Street. A perfect day.
>
> I remember looking out the window of the little maid's room where we had been installed, seeing the lights of the Palisades across the way, and thinking, *There! There it is! There's New York, this wonderful city. I'll go live there someday.* Even being in New York, the actual place, I found the idea of New York so wonderful that I could only imagine it as some other place, greater than any place that would let me sleep in it—a distant constellation of lights that I had not yet been allowed to visit. I had arrived in Oz only to think, *Well, you don't* live *in Oz, do you?*

That remains my fundamental experience with emigration, the notion of an other, shimmering place which remains an other, shimmering place while you remain in the dull and dirty and disappointing real place that they have put in its place as an attempt to switch things on you. Anne, you first saw New York

---

This transcript was adapted from a conversation that took place at the 2010 PEN World Voices Festival.

when, and under what circumstances?

ANNE LANDSMAN: I first saw New York City in 1981. My previous notions of America had been from the library that I'd grown up with—my parents had had a big collection of American-Jewish fiction, as well as a vinyl record called "You Don't Have to Be Jewish."

GOPNIK: This was a collection of Jewish jokes?

LANDSMAN: Yes, yes. I kind of grew up with this album, "You Don't Have to Be Jewish," and I learned from the record what an egg cream was. There was this character called James Bondstein, and he went into a deli and asked for an egg cream. That was the record I grew up with. I also grew up with Marjorie Morningstar—I guess that dates me, hugely.

GOPNIK: Herman Wouk's book. Marjorie was trying to pass—she grew up as Morningstern and she takes on Morningstar.

LANDSMAN: Right, she grew up on Central Park West and wanted to live in Greenwich Village. She falls in love with a very dashing playwright, Noel Airman. But eventually she marries the nice Jewish boy who her parents want her to marry. These were my fantasies of New York. And when I arrived it was a hot, dirty, difficult place. The first day, I remember I had a huge backpack and the place that I was supposed to stay—no one was there. I waited endlessly with my giant backpack and eventually, with five thousand quarters, called South Africa and spent the night at a friend of my mother's from way back when, Gloria Pelzig, who was a widowed New York City schoolteacher. I always think of Gloria Pelzig as my own personal Statue of Liberty. I spent the night in her apartment.

Many adventures later, I came to be a New Yorker again, to go to graduate school. In the section that I'll read from my novel *The Rowing Lesson*, the main character, Betsy Klein, lives in New York City and is visited by her father, Harry Klein. They're up on the roof of her loft on Bond Street. She's a painter, and she's just shown him some of her artwork in her studio. They're walking along on this tar-covered roof. He's a father from another place, another culture, and there's a big cultural difference now between father and daughter: He's been a country doctor in a small town in South Africa for most of his life and he's struggling to make sense of this daughter who's become something else. The novel is told in the second person, so the "you" is Betsy's voice, and the person she's talking to and about is her father:

You got up to look over the edge of the low, parapet wall. Somebody's going to have a terrible accident, you said, backing away. You know ever since my fall, my shoulder's never been the same. *Wragtig*, that was something. I was at Tjoekie van der Merwe's house, examining one of the kids who had chickenpox and I was just on my way out of the door. One minute I'm standing and the next minute I'm on my arse, twisted sideways, in their bloody conversation pit. I knew I'd fractured something. It hurt like hell. Your face was riven with melancholy, the hardest of memories. It's hard when an old person falls, you sighed. Old bones take a long time to heal and they're never the same again. Did you know I have Paget's disease?

What's that? I said airily, staring up at the empty sky.

My spine is turning into bamboo, for Chrissake!

Wait, you said, let me take a picture of you up here. You took your camera out of the old leather camera case around your neck. Stand over there, you told me. Not near the edge, for God's sake! Your mother wants lots and lots of pictures. Damn it. There's something wrong with the mechanism.

Dad! I said, waving my hand in front of my face. You're just like your mother. Impatient as hell. This camera is not as good as my old one. Hang on, chaps. Let's get those towers in the background. They look like giant tuning forks!

I was raised by parents who grew up on Damon Runyon stories. In this same novel, Betsy takes her father to see *Guys and Dolls* at the Martin Beck Theatre on 45th Street. He's ecstatic, because he's grown up in South Africa and the idea of seeing a Broadway play is thrilling to him. You have to hear in this section the sense of what it must have been like in the '40s, as South Africa was entering into a very different reality, to have Damon Runyon intersect with that.

Two nights before you left, I took you to see *Guys and Dolls* at the Martin Beck Theater on 45th Street, in the dazzling heart of the city. I wore big earrings, a swingy black dress, my hair pulled back. You sat tilted forward on the edge of your seat as Nathan Lane and Faith Prince sang and danced the Damon Runyon stories of your youth. Bloody marvelous! you said, turning to me at intermission, the high beams of your enthusiasm shining right at me. I can't believe I'm here, my girl. You did me a big favor. A wave of feeling spread across your features, black eyes softening, a rueful smile catching at me.

Harry the Horse! Nicely-Nicely Johnson! Mindy's Restaurant! Maxie knew pages and pages off-by-heart. Me and him and Mickey Levin used to go to…never mind. Before your time. Still, District Six was full of all kinds of characters. It's all gone now. Those bastards bulldozed the life out of Cape Town. Your mother and I saw it coming. It was not long after the war when the Nationalists came into power and the signs went up, Blankes, Nie-Blankes. Well it's all changing again. Who knows what's going to happen. It's bloody fascinating, though. I just hope I live long enough to see the verkramptes verkramped!

GOPNIK: It's wonderful to think that the American musical acts as such a beacon. Salman, I think of the wonderful essay you wrote about *The Wizard of Oz* and the making of your own mind. And *Guys and Dolls* acted similarly as an image of New York from a South African distance. José, you come from Cuba, originally.

JOSÉ MANUEL PRIETO: I think I am the newest immigrant here—I just came five years ago. I am from Cuba but I came to New York from Mexico, and before that I was living in Russia—so I am an immigrant of long experience. When I grew up in Cuba, we were enemies, Cuba and the United States, and the first time I came to this country I was very surprised. I wrote an article about this called "The Cuban Revolution Explained to Taxi Drivers," because I was so surprised by the popularity of the Cuban Revolution and Fidel Castro with taxi drivers in New York. I took the taxi all the time and they would say, "Where are you from?" "I am from Cuba." "Oh! Fidel Castro!" So I wrote an article trying to explain to them why I am not in much agreement with them. Growing up in Cuba, I was always reading American novels and that helped to shape my view of this country that was presented as our enemy. I wrote something about how literature helped me to figure out another idea, called *American Books I Read As a Child in Castro's Cuba.*

In the summer of 2007 I was invited to a dinner that *The Paris Review* organized in the city of New York in honor of Norman Mailer. The novelist had recently published what would be his last novel, *The Castle in the Forest*, and would hold a conversation with E.L. Doctorow. I went with the grand illusion of listening to these two greats of North American letters that would speak about their most recent books and their friendship of years. Nevertheless, what I did not yet know was that, thanks to the generosity of a friend, I shared the table with

Norman Mailer himself. So when I saw him enter the room and come up to our table with his very recognizable demeanor, that of a man once strapping and square, but who was now supporting himself with two canes, I could not help but become emotional. I stood up to greet him, and after responding to me with a rapid gesture of his head, he asked me to take his two canes (beautifully adorned with silver handles) from him and arrange them. He looked around. "There, by the window." Something which I did full of happiness. During the dinner that followed his electrifying dialogue with Doctorow, I had the opportunity to speak with him. I told him—what else do you say in these cases?—about my admiration for his books, which I began to read when very young, many years ago. At the center of the table were some copies of his novels, courtesy of the publishers, and I asked him to autograph a copy of *The Naked and the Dead*, which he kindly did. While he signed it, I mentioned to him how much reading this book in particular as a young person in Cuba had impacted me. He grumbled something, calculated in which year it ought to have been: "Yes, it's a powerful book for teens." And he autographed it for me plainly: "For José, from Norman Mailer."

That was all. About the dinner, nothing else was particularly memorable. I returned with that copy, which I placed next to the most precious books in my living room. Days later, I had some people over for dinner and I showed my friend the autographed copy. He asked me a question that left me a bit perplexed. "But how?" he said. "You read Norman Mailer in Cuba?" And added, "I would guess that North American writers were prohibited on the island." My friend had imagined, perhaps logically, that literature from the United States was not allowed to circulate in Cuba. I explained to him, passionately, that many books—even American books—had never been censored in Cuba. His commentary made me reflect, nonetheless, about the impact of the literature of our neighbors, the United States, and how close the borders of censorship and political mishaps were. I meditated also on the many books by American authors that I'd read as a child in Cuba, and the weight that literature had on my literary formation. Hemingway, William Faulkner, Carson McCullers, William Styron, Sherwood Anderson, and others. I was in an atmosphere of propaganda and indoctrination and literature helped me, like an antidote, not to be poisoned.

GOPNIK: Salman, like José, you're a kind of multiple immigrant: You came to the United States not simply from your original homeland of India, but by way of that Second World nation, England, and Great Britain. What were your first experiences and your first take on America? One of the things I'm noticing is that people have an image, an idea, implanted in their heads before they arrive here. Inevitably, it becomes a comparative moment.

SALMAN RUSHDIE: If I could begin by answering your Canadian belittlement with one in return: I remember Robin Williams saying that Canada was like this really beautiful apartment upstairs from a great party.

GOPNIK: But you know what people are doing in the upstairs apartment while the party is going on down there?

RUSHDIE: They hammer on the floor! Of course, one of the things about the all-pervasiveness of American culture is that you feel you know America before you ever come here. I grew up in Bombay listening to early rock and roll, Bill Haley and Elvis Presley. And those days, the movie theaters in Bombay, much more than they are now, were actually tied to Hollywood studios. There's a movie theater called The Metro which would show the MGM, first-release films, the musicals—*Seven Brides for Seven Brothers*, all that stuff. There was a cinema called The Empire which showed 20th Century Fox films, another called the Eros Cinema which showed Paramount films—so you had a very contemporary awareness of American cinema. And, of course, New York City is just so often represented that when you first come to New York, you have this odd double feeling that everything is familiar, but you don't know your way around. Every building you look at you think, "Oh sure, that one," but then you don't know where you're going. So that double familiarity-unfamiliarity was there for a lot of us, I'm sure.

I came in the early '70s, for the first time, into a very different New York City. I had a college friend from Cambridge, an American friend who had invited me to come and stay. When I knew him at Cambridge, he was rampantly heterosexual. In the meantime, since I'd last seen him, he had discovered that he was, in fact, rampantly homosexual. I remember my friend saying to me that this bar had just opened very, very high up in a building downtown and we should go there. "There's just one thing," he said. "You have to wear a suit and tie." And I said, "What, you have to wear a suit and a tie to go to a bar?" You know, I had long hair in those days, and a Zapata moustache. The idea of wearing a suit was against my religion. But he said, "No you should, it's really worth it." It was my first or second day in New York, and I was taken up to Windows on the World. That became an indelible early memory.

And, of course, that was such a different New York. It was dangerous. My uptown friends, when I told them I was staying on St. Mark's Place, they said, "Salman, you have to leave. Today." I said, "What? Because of the crack dealers at the doorstep?" And they said, "No, no, you don't understand. You have to move out. Now." Well, I didn't. Because of course the point about the crack dealers is that once they find out you don't have any money, they're fine. They're quite friendly.

GOPNIK: Like real estate brokers.

RUSHDIE: Yes. You had to learn these strange pathways through the city because there was a block that was safe and a block that wasn't and so you couldn't necessarily walk in a straight line to get across town without being mugged. Much later, when I came to live here—about eleven years ago now—I ended up writing a novel called *Fury*. It had the strange fate of being published on September 11th, 2001, and thus becoming a historical novel on the day it was published. And I know I'm not able to write about New York in the way that a native New Yorker might write about it, and I would not wish to try. But I thought I could write about the phenomenon of arrival. Because one of the things I think is remarkable about this city is how quickly it lets you become a New Yorker. You could be here a week—and a week later, your story is a New York story. I wanted to write about that New York—the New York of endless arrival.

> "Islam will cleanse this street of godless motherfucker bad drivers," the taxi driver screamed at a rival motorist. "Islam will purify this whole city of Jew pimp assholes like you and your whore roadhog of a Jew wife too." All the way up Tenth Avenue the curses continued. "Infidel fucker of your underage sister, the inferno of Allah awaits you and your unholy wreck of a motorcar as well." "Unclean offspring of a shit-eating pig, try that again and the victorious jihad will crush your balls in its unforgiving fist." Malik Solanka, listening in to the explosive, village-accented Urdu, was briefly distracted from his own inner turmoil by the driver's venom. ALI MAJNU said the card. Majnu meant *beloved*. This particular Beloved looked twenty-five or less, a nice handsome boy, tall and skinny with a sexy John Travolta quiff, and here he was living in New York, with a steady job; what had so comprehensively gotten his goat?
>
> Solanka silently answered his own question. When one is too young to have accumulated the bruises of one's own experience, one can choose to put on, like a hair shirt, the sufferings of one's world. In

this case, as the Middle East peace process staggered onward and the outgoing American president, hungry for a breakthrough to buff up his tarnished legacy, was urging Barak and Arafat to a Camp David summit conference, Tenth Avenue was perhaps being blamed for the continued sufferings of Palestine. Beloved Ali was Indian or Pakistani, but, no doubt out of some misguided collectivist spirit of paranoiac pan-Islamic solidarity, he blamed all New York road users for the tribulations of the Muslim world. In between curses, he spoke to his mother's brother on the radio—"Yes, Uncle. Yes, carefully, of course, Uncle. Yes, the car costs money. No, Uncle. Yes, courteously, always, Uncle, trust me. Yes, best policy. I know"—and also asked Solanka, sheepishly, for directions. It was the boy's first day at work in the mean streets, and he was scared witless. Solanka, himself in a state of high agitation, treated Beloved gently but did say, as he alighted at Verdi Square, "Maybe a little less of the blue language, okay, Ali Majnu? Tone it down. Some customers might be offended. Even those who don't understand."

The boy looked at him blankly. "I, sir? Swearing, sir? When?" This was odd. "All the way," Solanka explained. "At everyone within shouting distance. Motherfucker, Jew, the usual repertoire. *Urdu*," he added, in Urdu, to make things clear, "*meri madri zaban hai.*" Urdu is my mother tongue. Beloved blushed, deeply, the color spreading all the way to his collar line, and met Solanka's gaze with bewildered, innocent dark eyes. "Sahib, if you heard it, then it must be so. But, sir, you see, I am not aware." Solanka lost patience, turned to go. "It doesn't matter," he said. "Road rage. You were carried away. It's not important." As he walked off along Broadway, Beloved Ali shouted after him, needily, asking to be understood: "It means nothing, sahib. Me, I don't even go to the mosque. God bless America, OK? It's just words."

GOPNIK: Eduardo, we've heard about the idea of America as an antidote to propaganda. What was your first experience with the idea of America and then the reality that you encountered?

EDUARDO LAGO: In the other room, a few minutes ago, one of us said, "We are all immigrants." I said, "But I am not an immigrant." I still have not decided whether I am going to live in New York or not. It all began in 1985. I was traveling in Asia and every day, in the morning, I went for breakfast in the hotel in Kathmandu. There was a very big photograph of the Bay of Hong Kong. I was all by myself in the dining room, and I would say to myself, and I don't know why, "I think that one day I'm going to go to New York and live there." So that became very important to me, and in 1987, I took a leave of absence from my job as a teacher in Madrid, and I came to New York to try and understand that odd feeling. I had gone through a very difficult personal time; all inside myself I was totally crazy and nervous and anguished—and when I came to the city, this was the image that I had: Everything around me was madness and I was calm inside. I thought, "I have to live here." It felt right.

In the spring of '88, somebody who was the son of exiles from the Spanish Civil War, who was the dean of the City College, called me. He left a few messages on my answering machine, but I neglected him. One day he caught me and said, "Eduardo, normally people call me to ask favors. This is the first time I've had to call somebody three times to try and do *them* a favor. I have some friends who are writers. They told me I should try and help you since it doesn't make sense for you to go to Madrid. You should live in the city. And I think that you could do a PhD at the City University of New York. I think it would be wonderful for you." I left his office thinking, "Why would I do a PhD?" I was thirty-two or thirty-three. "Why would I want to study? I did that a long time ago. I want to continue with my own life in different ways—having fun, going out every single night, things like that." But he had said something to me. "If you are a good student, and you get your PhD, then you can live in New York." So for the sake of staying in New York, I decided to pursue my doctoral studies.

One day I was at Brooklyn College, where I was an adjunct teacher, about to finish my dissertation, and I got another phone call from the same guy. He said, "Eduardo, something very important happened. Can we make an appointment?" "What happened?" "I was doing the laundry yesterday in the basement of my building at Brooklyn Heights and I met with this person who is on the Committee at Sarah Lawrence College. You know Sarah Lawrence College, of course?" I said, "No, I don't. What is that?" It was June. "The Spanish teacher just resigned and they have nobody for the fall and they are desperate. Would you mind going there and meeting with them?"

So I spent a year there and I enjoyed the position very much. Then the woman who left the position decided to move permanently, and they gave me the position and later tenure. But to this day I remain a non-citizen. For reasons that would be very difficult for me to explain, although I have been writing since I was eight years old, I never wanted to publish. There is something about it that I don't like. The strong egos, the promotion, the market. There is something nauseating about that. So I wrote but never published. When I was fifty, I sent my novel to an agent in Barcelona. The novel was about New York mainly, but with some sections going back to Spain in the time of the civil war. It covers almost a century. She sent the novel out and it won a prestigious award.

GOPNIK: This is *Call Me Brooklyn?*

LAGO: Yes. So I went to see the dean, this was the same person, and I had to explain to her, "I won this award. I need to go to Spain to do the promotion. Can someone take care of my classes?" When I came back from the promotion, the Minister of Cultural Affairs from Spain said, "Eduardo, the current director of the Instituto Cervantes resigned and we thought of you." So, from the moment I saw that picture about going to Hong Kong to this moment, I haven't had the time to decide whether I want to live in New York or not.

GOPNIK: That's a wonderful story because I think that's what so many of us have experienced. Though we may think about living in New York, the reality of it is that it happens to us, rather than us happening to it. What I hear on the whole is a very positive vibe—that is, America, or at least New York, is a place of opportunity and self-transformation. The classic experience of people coming from the margins of the empire to the imperial capital is as much a tradition of exile, of feelings of alienation and loss as it is of opportunity. Is something different about the American experience, or are we all being a little polite about the degree of exile and alienation that we experience?

RUSHDIE: I don't know about the American experience, but New York, I think, is different, in the way that the great city is often different than the country it is in. London is not like England; Paris is not like France; New York is not like America. I wanted to live in New York, I didn't want to live in America. It's always reminded me of Bombay. Even Manhattan Island is about the size and shape of what is now called South Bombay, which used to be Bombay. As that young man arriving here in my twenties, I had a deep instinct that I should put myself in this place. It was a long time before I was able to do that, but from that moment in my twenties I felt a great attraction.

LANDSMAN: I completely connect with that. I suppose for me there's an excitement about this cultural diversity that never goes away. There was an article on the front page of *The New York Times* this week about the fact that there are more than eight hundred languages spoken in New York City. To this day I read an article like that with a thrill. Coming from apartheid South Africa, when I was growing up there were such harsh divides. Not to say that New York is the integrated place that we would like it to be, but the notion that there are eight hundred languages spoken in these five boroughs is still thrilling. There were moments when all of you were talking that I had connections: I also lived on St. Mark's Place, for instance. But, you know, there are still moments of alienation. I came from a place of real political challenge but great natural beauty. So when I first came to New York I kept looking for the mountains behind the skyscrapers. I kept thinking, "There are the buildings, but where are the mountains?" Cape Town is extraordinary in that way. In the little town where I grew up, seventy-two miles north of Cape Town, there were always mountains. I just assumed every city had some kind of mountains. I think Naipaul calls it "the second language of the eyes": When I'm confronted with a natural landscape I yearn for my own native flora and fauna. I don't have that problem in New York City because I'm not confronted with the natural landscape.

GOPNIK: Is there something fundamentally different about coming from a Hispanic background? In two senses: one, the long history in Cuba and South America of enmity and oppression might give you a different take on the American reality; and two, as you've written about, José, New York is in so many ways a Spanish-speaking city.

PRIETO: For me, to be in New York is to be in a place where I can travel between all the places I used to live. There is a big Russian community in Brighton Beach. In one day I can be in Russia or in Mexico—all of the places at the same time. My wife is from Russia, and when I used to live in Mexico with my family, I would travel to New York and bring back many Russian foods. I also come from a part of Latin America where the Spanish you speak, people from other Spanish-speaking countries understand you. So it's very comfortable here.

LAGO: I owe something very big to New York: the fact that I am a published writer. I don't think it would have happened elsewhere. So there is something in this city that I received instantly. The image of madness around me could be translated into some kind of sheer, pure, wonderful energy. Just like John Steinbeck said, after living in New York, "no place is good enough." That is very true. I also recall a sentence from Gabriel García Márquez. When they asked him about immigration and the language, he said, "We didn't come to the United States, the United States came to us."

GOPNIK: Came to Colombia as an oppressive presence, you mean?

LAGO: Came to Latin America, yes. In 1848 Mexico ceded half of its national territory to the United States. That's why there are places named San Francisco, California, Nevada, Colorado, and so on. The first text ever written in what is now the national territory of the United States was written by a Spanish chronicler, Gaspar Pérez de Villagrá, in the 1600s. When the Treaty of Guadalupe Hidalgo was signed in 1848, enormous parts of the population that only spoke Spanish became part of the landscape. The Spanish language is not and has never been a foreign language in the United States. Because of the strength of the influx of immigration, now over a quarter of the population speaks Spanish, and many of them only Spanish. This is a very complex issue. We published a book which is only in Spanish right now: *The Encyclopedia of Spanish in the United States*. It is a twelve-hundred-page volume. Eighty scholars contributed to it. It's the history of movies, of theater, and so on. There is a huge, huge wealth of history. The history of the United States has not been written entirely correctly because it has been written exclusively from the point of view of Anglo Saxons.

GOPNIK: From Massachusetts on in.

LAGO: Right. And look at all the missions in California.

GOPNIK: So part of your experience is coming to a place where the history needs to be rewritten because it has been written over, so to speak. It's fascinating—in my own family history, like that of so many people, this place was seen as a golden land where they felt they were connecting to the history of the rulers. That is, they could go to Ivy League colleges and then take on, to some degree and with whatever ambiguity, the identity of the overclass. But something else occurs to me as we're talking here, and that is the gift of anonymity that New York provides for all of us. Maybe it speaks to what you were saying, Eduardo, about being able to write here, that you're not defined every moment and at every turn by your class, or clan, or cohort identity. I remember, Salman—you probably don't—seeing you for dinner when you'd just moved to New York, and we'd seen each other in Europe over the previous ten years fairly often. It had been a very difficult and oppressive—famously so—time of your life. And I had the sense that when we stepped into a taxi cab in New York you were breathing freely for the first time, with no disguise, either overt or interior.

RUSHDIE: Yes. Although, as we were saying, most of the taxi drivers are from those countries. I've never had a problem here, I have to say. I think also of the influence of Jewish-American literature. When I read Roth, Bellow, Malamud, and others, I noticed the ease with which they were prepared to include other languages in an English text. Yiddish, for example. Often I didn't know what these words were. In *Portnoy's Complaint*, Portnoy, at a certain point, receives what is described as "a zetz in the kishkas." I'm thinking, "Zetz, kishkas? What are they?" You could see from the context that it was some kind of assault, rather than a spice or a thing to eat. And I remember it gave me a kind of permission, because I was trying to write in English about India, where people are also polyglot and where all kinds of words leak into English from other languages. Obviously you can't do it on the page quite as freely as you would in real life because the languages get too jumbled. But it just loosened something up in me. I thought, "As long as I can make things clear from context, so people can see whether it's something to eat or a swear word or whatever—as long as that's clear, then why not?" The way I went on to write *Midnight's Children* was certainly helped by reading those writers.

LANDSMAN: I find that fascinating. When I think how American fiction influenced me, it's actually writers like Salman Rushdie that come to mind. There's a sort of chain. I've come to feel that it's OK to use Afrikaans. In a way, being in a place where people are taking these chances, bringing in strands of their own traditions, is really liberating. For me, the excitement isn't about reading the writers you think of as "Great American Writers" in some traditional sense, but reading writers who bring in their own languages.

LAGO: There are, I think, Spanish writers whose work is not in Spanish but in English. The most obvious case is Junot Díaz, but there are many, many others— like Oscar Hijuelos, who won the Pulitzer Prize eighteen years before. This whole range of literature has originated in the United States in an incredible way. When my novel was published in France last year, the critic from *Le Monde* said, "Eduardo Lago has no connection with the Hispanic tradition. He is not a Hispanic writer. He's an American writer who writes about New York in Spanish."

PRIETO: The tradition of writing in a foreign language about living in New York is very long. We have the famous Cuban writer from the nineteenth century, Jose Martí, who was a national hero. He wrote very interesting chronicles about New York. The other day a restaurant was reopened in the Village where he used to go. The place was also well known because Oscar Wilde used to go there, and Mark Twain. The other day I went with my translator, Esther Allen, and we spoke with people there. We told them, "You know this place is also related to the famous writer José Martí?" But they didn't know. Martí is very important to me; he was an inspiration for coming here. His chronicles are well translated into English. I am writing a novel now that takes place in nineteenth-century New York, and so I read his chronicles recently, and I found them to be wonderful.

LAGO: In September they are going to open an exhibition in the Museum of the City of New York and El Museo del Barrio which is titled *Nueva York*. People are going to be shocked. The history of Hispanic New York begins in the seventeenth century with the Sephardic Jews.

AUDIENCE: I am a Spanish playwright. Why is it that if you are a foreigner then you have to talk about tradition, roots, all that kind of stuff? But if you are an Anglo-Saxon American writer you only have to talk about your individual writing and you don't have to go on this "tradition" route.

GOPNIK: I don't know if that's true. I'm not sure who the Anglo Saxon writer would be, but the late, much missed John Updike, for instance—one of the things that he was very concerned with was what kind of WASP he was. He was a poor, Dutch, white guy. He was not in touch with the New England tradition, but with the Pennsylvanian.

RUSHDIE: To speak for myself, when I wrote *Fury*, I was, in fact, writing an anti-tradition novel. I was writing about what happened the day before yesterday. It was a deliberate risk to write a novel about the exact moment in which the novel was being written. And to make it—if I did it right—more than just journalism. Whereas other times when I've written I've been very aware of heritage and tradition and so on.

LAGO: Adam asked me why I am not yet a citizen. It's very complicated, but I think now I know why. I would apply for New York citizenship, not for American citizenship. In terms of the writing, I think that nowadays, here, there is a huge amount of energy. Writers are renovating literature in a way that isn't happening in other places. There are great writers from India, from the diaspora, et cetera. But here there is a laboratory of ideas. And that is refreshing for anyone who writes. I think many of the best things that are happening in fiction these days are happening here.

RUSHDIE: I think we've been speaking affectionately about this city because we chose to live here, because we liked it. But I think it would be wrong to deduce that this is some kind of unique "City on the Hill," a New Jerusalem. I love other cities, too. I really love London, and I think it's every bit as cosmopolitan—but in a different way.

LAGO: What I've heard about New York is that every single day you find someone who is much more intelligent than you. Richer, better, everything. It is a lesson in humility. You find these wonderful people and that makes you much richer. And that is certainly true of writers. I meet writers every day who enrich me continuously. And I don't think that that is happening in Paris. I doubt it.

RUSHDIE: I think it's true that one of the delights of New York City is this enormous proliferation of subcultures. But I think it may be a little too easy to think that there is not a ruling class. There is a ruling class. It's a city dominated by money and power. It is not a class system in a way that the English or the Europeans might recognize, but that doesn't mean that there isn't one. There are "Masters of the Universe" here.

GOPNIK: Meritocracies produce classes as much as hereditary societies. I guess what you're saying here, Eduardo, is that you don't have to be a narrow, insular patriot of New York to recognize that there is usually one cosmopolitan center. Paris played that role from 1789 to 1950; wherever you were from, whether you were James Joyce or Samuel Beckett, or coming from the French provinces, you washed up in Paris and you remade yourself as a person, you found yourself. Paris, a city I dearly love and where I lived for many years, doesn't play that role now. It's a polyglot city, increasingly, but it's not a cosmopolitan city in that particular sense. I don't think you have to be a New York chauvinist to think that it has been one of the features of Western civilization to have a cosmopolitan center that changes from century to century, sometimes from generation to generation, and to recognize that from at least 1950 to today as we are speaking, it is New York.

PRIETO: The feeling of cosmopolitanism is very important. I have met readers from many other countries here, and publishers who understand Latin American literature, or literature from other countries. Although it is true that few translated books are published in English, on the other hand you have specialists in every type of literature here. People here are paying attention to what is happening all around the world.

RUSHDIE: We're using this word "cosmopolitan" as if it was an unarguably good thing. But in recent years there has been more than one discourse that uses it pejoratively. Certainly in Marxist discourse cosmopolitanism was problematic because it was related to deracination, it was related to things that were not necessarily good. I don't want to get into postcolonial theory, but the uprooting of a writer from native soil can be in some way diminishing, and this urban experience of people living in cities by choice and writing about wherever they want—there may be something wrong with that. I think we need to understand that there is a problematic aspect of it.

LANDSMAN: That's interesting. I read an article in *The Independent* saying that South Africa was the featured country at the London Book Fair. They listed all the South African writers, new writers dealing with different issues than we dealt with in apartheid South Africa. And then they mentioned a group of South African writers who write about South Africa, writers like myself, who live outside the country. The last line was, "It's questionable how South African they are." When you leave the country of your birth, does that original sense of rootedness drain out of you? I've been struggling with this idea, so I turned to Eudora Welty's piece "Place in Fiction." She talks about how "the home tie is the blood tie." For me that does still feel true, that there's an incredible connectedness.

At this World Voices Festival, I was on a panel with Siri Hustvedt, and I asked her, "You've been coming back between here and Norway and you speak Norwegian. Do you feel Norwegian-American?" She said, "As I get older I feel more Norwegian." So, again, it's a question both of how people label you and how you see yourself. It's tricky and awkward. Certainly in regard to South African fiction at the moment, people are dealing with difficult social and political ills on the ground. And I'm here with a different perspective, often a historical perspective, or a perspective that goes somewhere else completely. Luckily South Africans have been very generous with my work and have welcomed it. But there is that constant nagging question, "Do you lose? Does the sense of who you are leave you over time?"

RUSHDIE: There's a discourse in Indian literature about the difference between the Indian writers who live in India and those who live abroad. There's a constant polemic about it which varies in heat at different times. I remember being at a dinner given for a group of Indian writers at a literary festival, and an Indian woman writer, whom I will not name, sitting next me, suddenly, apropos of nothing, leaned to me and said, "Of course your position in Indian literature is highly problematic."

GOPNIK: This was with the first course?

RUSHDIE: And I said, really? And she said, "Yes, highly."

AUDIENCE: Trying to bring this back full circle: You began by talking about the dream of New York versus the reality of New York. It seems to me that there are a lot of people for whom New York is a dual reality. There's the reality of the rich and the poor, the reality of the beautiful and the grungy.

RUSHDIE: I would say that's true of every city. It exists partly as a practical matter you have to deal with every day and partly in your mind. There is no question that New York is one of the most annoying cities to live in at the level of interacting with its official manifestations. It's unbelievably difficult. How hard it is to deal with the business of life in New York. It infuriates me. It's perfectly possible to trash the place, but the fact is, for me, that I wake up in the morning, I go to the corner, I buy the paper and a cup of coffee and I am in a good mood. It isn't anything more complicated than that. I like it. So the stuff I don't like, I don't like, but the dream city is still there.

LANDSMAN: I think again of what Eduardo said about how a person with a lot of inner turmoil comes to a city with a lot of outward turmoil and feels at peace. I found a real kinship with that statement.

LAGO: One day I was with a friend from Spain and he said, "How can you deal with such an ugly city?" And I looked around and said, "Is it ugly?" I realized he was right—and the weather is bad, too. But nobody leaves.

FICTION

THE DECISION

Quim Monzó

Translated by Mary Ann Newman

In the evening, the femme fatale and the irresistible man meet up in a café with ochre walls. They look into each other's eyes. They know that this time is the last time. For a few weeks now, the fragility of the thread that had held them together for the past three years, and that led them to call each other at all hours, to live for each other (so great was their fascination that not even Sunday afternoons were boring), has begun to be evident to both of them. Now, the thread is about to break. The moment to question the love they feel for each other and, thus, to part company, has arrived.

Before, they used to see each other every day, and the day they didn't see each other, they called, even if they were in the middle of a conference in Nova Scotia. The last few weeks they've barely been together three times, and those haven't been happy meetings. Without need of saying it, they both know that today's meeting is for the purpose of saying an implacable goodbye. They have reached such a degree of mutual understanding that neither of them must spell out the fact that they're bored, because the two of them realize it simultaneously. They take each other by the hand and remember (each to himself, in silence) the fornicary perfection they had achieved toward the end; they themselves are amazed. It's not at all strange that, in contrast with such acrobatics, the rest of their lives should seem dull to them. They have coffee, say goodbye, and go their own ways. She has arranged to have dinner with a man; he has arranged to have dinner with a woman.

After dessert, within an hour and a half the femme fatale is in bed with the man she had dinner with. It takes three hours for the irresistible man to get into bed with his partner. They find themselves doing it so clumsily that they are thrilled. What passivity! What awkwardness! What anxiety! What impatience! They have a long way to go with their new lovers before they reach the perfection to which they have just bade farewell, that evening, over coffee.

TÍTÍLOLÁ

Akinwumi Isola

Translated by Akinloyé A. Òjó

It's not that I have never seen a bird,
But the peacock is different among birds.
It's not that I have never seen a snake before,
But Nìnì is the most attractive of snakes.
Even though non-human,
It covers itself in the farm with velvet.
It's not that I have never seen spinach,
But òpòpò has the most attractive texture to me.
It stands out with its cool dark texture,
The eye that has seen masquerades and festivals
But that has not seen the Gèlèdé performance
Has really not seen anything.
It's not that I have never seen a young woman,
But the day I briefly saw Títí
Was when I concurred that the work of God is limitless.
Beauty could be in twenty ways.
Beauty could be in thirty ways.
But beauty is different from beauty,
Congenital is different from fashioned,
The natural is different from cosmetic.
Títí is exceptionally beautiful,
She stands out among others.
To be dark-complexioned and shiny too!
To walk and walk gorgeously.
Clear eyes as fresh as the water in the mud pot
Thighs as sweet as a comb of honey.
If you claim to be as beautiful as Títí

Your character cannot be as good as Títí's,
And even if you say you have good character
Your intelligence cannot be close to that of my friend.
Equitable body, desirably slim
With hair-like-a-crown, her teeth, white as cotton.
If a wise person has character and beauty
She cannot but be highly attractive all over.
The-knowledge-is-forever,
The-character-is-forever,
The-beauty-is-forever,
The-wealth-is-forever.
And so, what is wrong
That you close your ears to my song?
Open your ears, my song is sweet
It is indeed harmonious.
You own the house where I want to dwell,
You own the door that I am knocking.
Don't hide your love,
Open the door for me,
I want to enter.

ÀJOKÉ

Akinwumi Isola

Translated by Akinloyé A. Òjó

If you see a man fetching fire with his bare hands,
Please don't scorn him; he has something he wants to do.
Maybe he wants to smoke a pipe,
Maybe he wants to roast kókóró,
He may want to burn the house of the person who took his wife.
I have seen a person who walked, walked, and walked until he ran into a train!
He wasn't blind, neither was he crippled,
He got into trouble watching a crowd dealing with a petty thief.
The able-bodied man that took off in the middle of Ojàaba market,
Don't chastise him,
He doesn't have his resident permit and he doesn't want to go to jail.
I was walking in the market, I ran into the cloth seller's stall,
The cloth seller struck me with a staff across my backside.
I rubbed the spot and I endured.
It doesn't hurt me.
It really doesn't hurt me; I know what I am doing.
The mother of the twins is not crazy,
She is only dancing for her children.
You might strike me with a cane, not only a staff,
It was the black and shiny maiden that I was looking at
when I walked into the cloth seller's stall.
I cannot but look at the black and shiny maiden,
I cannot but look at the backside of beads.
It is not possible to look at the teeth that make the mouth perfect
in the market without running into the cloth seller's stall.
If the eye beholds a faultless beauty,
It will blink continuously.

If one sees an impeccable being
One can become confused.
A set of eyes are not enough,
Even two sets of eyes are not enough to see the wonder,
The wonder that I am viewing,
The wonders that I am viewing on my friend,
My friend that is beautiful-as-the-dawn
Gentle-natured as the dove,
That is perfect without any blemish.
It seems that Obàtálá was sound awake,
He wasn't sleepy the day he made Àjoké,
Àjoké looks tender, she is well proportioned
And she looks luscious.
She makes me long after her.
She is as silky as Òdú,
The Òdú on new soil.
Àjoké has the basket of character for her beauty.
As I look at the beauty, I crave the character,
As I behold the face,
Two hundred thoughts go through my mind.
The Almighty God who has blessed Àjàgbé with this
Is the One that ordained joy to collide with happiness
Children will acquire the beauty from us.

OLÁNÍKÈÉ

Akinwumi Isola

Translated by Akinloyé A. Òjó

If you ask me to speak
my comrades,
I, the-one-with-the-honeyed-lips, the-one-with-words-below-the-navel
I can go on like this till tomorrow, all fresh and new
Because of my dear one:
Clear-eyes-as-the-dove,
one-with-beaming-smiling-teeth,
Well-proportioned,
Beautiful-as-the-new-day,
The dimpled cheeks form the groove of the body!
If we speak up, it will seem like an adage,
And if we don't speak, it might seem like a fight,
I had chosen not to speak on countless instances
For it is not everything that the eyes see
That the mouth can speak about,
If we decide to speak about the beautiful maidens
All around this land,
One would have no other vocation
Except to sing for them all.
However, salt is unique among all cooking ingredients,
The uniqueness of Àlà's clothes is clear among clothes,
If kolanuts are twenty, and there are thirty gbànja
Their internal parts are going to be viewed variously.
The day seemed like yesterday
That I caught a glimpse of the gorgeous among beings,
Oláníkèé, the one with-legs-like-a-shimmering-bunch-of-beads,
Rhythmic backside with hands like pillars of silver,
The headgear didn't allow me to quickly see the lengthy hair,

Long hair that she weaved in corn-rows,
Cheeks full of beaming smiles.
White teeth as the emergence of fresh cotton.
Faultless are the dancing steps of the meticulous,
Pleasing are the walking steps of the beautiful
Oláníkèé, soft are the words of a real child.
All these make you honorable.
You are the one that says I should speak,
I had wanted to keep quiet,
But how can one see something like this,
then cover one's mouth?
It is as a blessing that God has made you for this land,
I want to care for the exceptional body.
The Àlà cloth that the Òrisa worshipper craves,
Oláníkèé, I crave you more than the àlà cloth.
If the eye beholds a unique person,
The image lingers longer in the brain.
Oláníkèé, at all times,
My inner eye perceives you.

FICTION

AMONG THE MISSING

Linor Goralik

Translated by Peter Golub

LITTLE LENAS

"And here is another little Lena!" he said, nudging the girl forward and simultaneously blocking the space between the juice aisle and the soda pop aisle—making it impossible for her to pass them. The girl immediately hid her face in her father's jeans. She was a thick plump little girl who looked nothing like her father.

"A brilliant girl," he said. "She's only a year and eight months, and can you imagine, she sings, dances, and can count to ten!"

She just stood there smiling, tightly gripping the handle of her shopping cart. Stood, smiled, waited for him to move his little Lena out of her way.

"Lena, sweetie, won't you give us a count down? Oh come on, don't be shy!" He lightly pulled on one of the girl's wilted pigtails; the child mumbled something indecipherable, and proceeded to kick a large sticker on the floor, advertising discounted tableware.

"She is a brilliant girl," he repeated with a tinge of disappointment in his voice. She continued to stand and smile. The place where she held the cart was moist and warm. He waved the hand not directly placed on the little Lena. "OK then, it was good to see you. You look great, as always."

She didn't answer, just smiled even wider. He quickly lifted his little Lena into his arms, put her in the shopping cart, with the little fat legs facing him, and rolled off in the opposite direction.

Only then did she close her eyes and call upon her Black Angels, ordering them to tear him into tiny pieces that very night, and to take the little Lena to a frozen mountain to be fed to a pack of wolves. The Angels humbly bowed, kneeling on the ground before her. She took a bottle of mineral water off the shelf, and began drinking it right there and then, while the Angels pushed her cart to the meat department.

Peter Golub's translation of Linor Goralik was supported in part by the PEN Translation Fund.

JUST IN CASE
For G.&G.

He said they needed to talk, but that they couldn't do it at his house or her house, not at his office or the smoke room at her dead-end job, not anywhere where there were ears or even walls. It was almost minus thirty degrees. They ran to a twenty-four hour pharmacy, and there, toying with a plastic bag which held a small colorful monster to be used as a bath sponge, he told her that in the near future she would hear things about him that she should not believe. "Or rather," he said while squeezing one of the monster's claws, "believe whatever you want, just promise me that you'll let me explain everything, that you'll come to me so that I can explain everything, and then you can believe whatever you want. If I can't convince you…then it's done—believe whatever you want."

"Jesus! What's wrong?" she asked. She began to pull the plastic bag toward her, unable to bear the sight of the claws being contorted by the torture, their fragile crunching, the exposed white thread of the stitching. But he did not relent, and tightly clung to the bag. "Who can tell me what? What's the mystery? What's going to happen?"

"There is a chance," he said.

"OK," she said, and again tugged at the plastic bag. "OK, just tell me for Christ's sake, are you in trouble. Are you in some kind of danger? Is there a chance something terrible is going to happen? What? What's going on?"

At this point he suddenly looked at her as if only then considering all the possibilities. Then he put a finger inside the bag and scratched the monster behind the ear. "No, no. Of course not. Nothing is going to happen."

DOESN'T COUNT

He rubbed his temples with his middle finger and thumb. She asked, "Your head hurt?" He lowered it in response. Then she said, "If you like, I can kiss it, and then everything will pass?" He looked up, surprised, and stared at her. She quickly looked away, and made an awkward wave of the hand, as if trying to move the words out of the air between them, and hastily left the elevator.

NO SLEEP

He got up off the floor, and, abhorring all existence, went to open the door. The doorway was instantly flooded with water. He looked with derision at the late-night guest—a boy, probably fourteen or fifteen, soaked through, wiping his face with his palm, cradling a half-dead bouquet at an odd angle, the way someone would hold a baby. He considered the possibility that the boy was a courier from a flower delivery service, lost, come to the wrong address.

"What?!" he snapped at the boy. The boy, trying to clumsily shield the crumbling bouquet with his coat, yelled through the roar of the water:

"...forgive me, sir! I know it's very late! It's just that! My bus, sir! It was the earliest I could catch, so I've arrived only now! I'm Samuel. Samuel Weis! I have come to see Irine, sir! I need to speak to her! I am her friend from that school, the one in Essex, sir! I was able to catch a bus only at four-twenty-six! Sir, I am sorry for being so late!"

"There is no Irine here!" he yelled back.

"What?" yelled the boy. He again repeated what he said, but this time almost closing the door so that the water would not wet the rug:

"There is no Irine here!"

"Irine Lowell, sir!" the boy yelled back.

"Lowell left two months ago!" he yelled back. "I don't know where she is. I suggest you try the post office!"

He shut the door and tightly bolted it, returned to the drawing room, sat on the floor near the couch, and carefully lifted the lampshade, illuminating a small area of the room. The cat breathed heavily and hoarsely, its mangy side rose and fell from time to time as it moaned in an almost human voice. In anguish, the cat pressed its paw against its stomach, inside which resided excruciating pain. The shot obviously didn't help. He put his hand over the cat's forehead, and thought that this probably caused it even more pain, and again lowered the lampshade. He thought that perhaps they should take the cat with them, and not leave it with the sale of the house; perhaps, there at the new place, it would keep living and living. He thought that perhaps they shouldn't leave at all: Irine would go to the door, and for a few minutes she would look at the fool with the flowers, and then say: "My cat is dying." Then they would sit next to it until morning, and sooner or later awkwardly kiss, and then everything wouldn't be so unbearable.

IT'S GOING TO BE OK

"Please," she said in a broken monotone, "Please put the knife away," and at that moment the quivering blade touched her neck. She began to hyperventilate from the fear, and wanted to lunge back, but she was pressed against the wall and tried to press as hard as she could against it.

They stood like that for a few seconds. He tried not to look at her, and ran his gaze over the unfamiliar kitchen. Watching him, she thought that this is how people scan a room when searching for a place to hide.

"Please," she said, trying not to move her throat. "I'll do..."

"Undress!" he yelled.

She ran her stiff fingers over the collar of her shirt, deathly afraid of catching her throat on the shaking knife. She managed to find the tip of the zipper and pulled it down to about the middle of her back and involuntarily dropped it.

Suddenly he began to cry. First quietly, trying to hide his face behind the arm that still held the knife, and then he began to sob, folding onto the floor. She gathered him in her arms and together with him sat on the floor in an awkward position against the wall. He fell into her lap. He was skinny and very light. "Perhaps," she thought, "he's older than I thought. Perhaps, he's twelve or even thirteen." He pressed his wet face against her clavicle and she began to mumble that everything was OK, that no one will find out, that he shouldn't cry. Because of the extremely uncomfortable position against the wall her back began to ache. A draft blew in from the broken window, and they sat there like that until they were nearly freezing.

JULIETTE

He did not hear her enter the room, but he could sense the smell of her perfume, strong, sweet, almost meretricious, extravagant; his lips began to ache. She had considered everything; there was very little light, even the blinds were carefully drawn, and he could barely see her silently approaching him, a dark figure on a dark background. He outstretched his hand, but she roughly grabbed his wrists, and the contact of the cool black satin gloves seemed to him rather vulgar. He involuntarily flexed his legs, exhaled, and gave into her, and she began to slowly move her gloved hand along his chest, his stomach, cruelly stopping at his belly button. He impatiently raised his knees, but she made no response to this gesture; although, she did kneel lower and he greedily breathed in the warm scent of her soft, perfectly round, expanding, corseted breasts. She kneeled even lower, and he could no longer contain his desire, grabbing her thigh, attempting to press his fingers under the thick lace band holding up her stockings. He promptly received a satin glove across the lips. The space between him and the breasts instantly increased and the hand caressing his stomach withdrew. He learned the lesson and dolefully quieted, and was forgiven. He was allowed to remove a satin glove with his teeth and greedily wrap his fingers around a thin finger with a short slightly serrated nail.

He moaned from pleasure when the finger stroked his tongue. She carefully kicked one leg over him and stood above him on her knees, and he managed to catch another smell under the perfume, a human sexual smell, and, bending, he tried to touch his body to hers, but she did not hurry, lowering slower and slower and then pressed her hands into the pillow behind his head, and fell to her side, rolling to the wall. He tried to catch his breath, found the remote in the bedside table, and turned on the light. She moaned and tried to block the light with her palm.

"Sweetie?" he asked. "What's wrong? Love?"

"It just doesn't help," she said. "It just doesn't. I know, I know I thought it all up myself and now please forgive me. I just don't feel better after all this, this regalia. Forgive me. Forgive a ridiculous old floozy, that's how I feel right now."

DRAMA

BRIGHTEST NOON

Dea Loher

Translated by Daniel Brunet

1

At noon on the nineteenth of August two thousand and
At brightest noon on the nineteenth of August two thousand and
It was the August before
It's already a few years ago
The light that August
Was blindingly bright
The light that August
Made the outlines of the objects houses trees cars
And people themselves
Appear as clearly as if they had been cut out

At brightest noon of the such and such of August a few years ago
A stranger entered our neighborhood
He was so strange
That he didn't look around
And didn't look to the right or left
He went down the street
In the middle of the lane
To Nelli's bar
And instead of going inside
He remained standing in front of it
On the sidewalk
Where a boy named
Silence.

Daniel Brunet's translation of Dea Loher was supported in part by the PEN Translation Fund.

Where the eight-year-old
Pause. Very quietly.
Edgar
Pause.
When an eight-year-old boy helplessly
Looks at his soccer ball
As it lies softly between his hands
Is the valve leaking
The boy looks at the stranger
The stranger puts down his duffle bag and takes the ball, turns it, examines the
    valve
The two don't need any more words than that

At brightest noon of the such and such of August a few years ago
Olaf the bird drives out of the coke oven with a stolen car
With a borrowed, borrowed, only borrowed
With a car, that doesn't belong to him
At an otherworldly speed
He almost flew
Past the stranger and the boy
Standing absorbed in a soccer ball
In front of Nelli's bar
Olaf the coke bird rocket
At brightest noon an eight-year-old boy became so startled that

Where whoa driving in the direction or whoa tracks train train station
In the light of that August
Nothing else in mind but the fleeing danger and hold
Doggedly surprised scared
Tight to the coke rocket
And now
As Edna sees the boy in the cloud of dust
Appearing as a shadow in front of the sun
Directly in front of her
There

The street
Empty of people
The heat
We didn't see it

We weren't present
But there is him
The sole
Eyewitness

2

Susanne washes her mother-in-law in the tub with a sponge. Slowly. Very lovingly.

FRAU SCHRAUBE   Where is little Edgar. He hasn't come to see me yet today.

SUSANNE   Little Edgar is dead, Rosmarie.

FRAU SCHRAUBE   Dead—since when. *(Pause.)* But he was still so little. Why did he die. *(Tries to remember.)* Where is. How old is. What year is it. What year—

SUSANNE   Lift your arm. High.

FRAU SCHRAUBE   Where is—

LUDWIG   Edgar's on a school trip. With his whole class.

Susanne looks at him in astonishment.

FRAU SCHRAUBE   Oh. *(Pause.)* And they're staying overnight. *(Pause.)* Then he'll be back soon.

LUDWIG   Yes, mama, he'll be back soon.

Pause

FRAU SCHRAUBE   Where did they go.

Pause. Ludwig gives Susanne a sign.

SUSANNE   To the sea. They're at the Wadden Sea. Ebb and flow. That's what they're learning right now, the tides. How to build dams, how to extract salt. Mussels snails fish. Where life comes from. How the swells and the beach change, every day. Why the sea is always eating up more land. How to make the water clean again. After an accident.

FRAU SCHRAUBE Oh, the oil. The oil burns in the eyes.

Susanne dries her off.

SUSANNE Here are your memory cards, Rosmarie. I'm putting them next to the laundry.

ROSMARIE Not now. It's better to lie in bed without a bunch of papers.

SUSANNE They're for tomorrow morning. Remind me to remind you.

ROSMARIE If I don't forget.

They laugh. Rosmarie goes to bed.

LUDWIG You're wearing a belt. Your stockings are falling down. You're washing the laundry at one hundred degrees to shrink your clothes. You should eat.

SUSANNE I don't want to. I can't. I don't want to eat anything anymore that has a heart.

LUDWIG (*Sighs.*) Susanne—

SUSANNE It has to go on. Doesn't it. The piano has to be played. The bread has to be cut. The heart has to beat.

LUDWIG Then just rice. Eggs—

SUSANNE The day has to break. Money has to be earned. The heart has to beat.

LUDWIG	I'll make a list. *(Silence.)* I wish I knew what I should do. How to help us. But no one can tell me that.
SUSANNE	Ideas want to be born. The heart has to beat.
LUDWIG	A small, rough pebble in a stream, that's what you are. The water will need millennia to make you smooth.
SUSANNE	Did you hear about the man who saw how Edgar was thrown into the air and left lying on the street. Do you know what he did—
LUDWIG	Yes, of course. Everyone knows.
SUSANNE	So. Everyone knows. *(Pause.)*
LUDWIG	I try not to count the days. And to go on. Just go on.

3

Then we learned the name of the stranger
His name is Rabe
Rabe what was it
Meier Rabe Meier
Wait, what's first and what's last
Rabe first name, Meier last name

Then we questioned the stranger
We questioned him, before we knew his name
Or anything else
About him
He rented a room
Three minutes after the accident
He rented a room
And disappeared inside it
And we heard him scream
He screamed the entire afternoon and the evening

He screamed all through the night and he screamed the next day
The day the night the day
Screaming, what does that mean
His screaming sounded like someone falling from a very high place
From a steep cliff, maybe, from a forty-two story skyscraper
From the tip of a tower or from a cable car
And he has to relive the fall again, barely after it's over
Again and again
Sentenced to fall and fall and fall with unending fear
We waited
Rabe Meier screamed
We sent for the doctor
She went upstairs and inside and found Rabe sitting on the bed
The bed sheets full of blood stains
He had, while he screamed, filed his nails
The afternoon the night the day
Longer than twenty-four hours
He filed them with an iron file
The nails had turned to dust
No more flesh at the tips
He scraped away both, nail and flesh, down to the bare bones
They bandaged his hands
Wrapped a gauze bandage around each individual finger

Gave him something to help him sleep
And something else for the pain
And he was supposed to stay there
In the small room, dark
With closed curtains
Would he ever open them

Yes
Said the stranger
Yes yes I saw everything
I was there Yes Yes Everything everything saw everything

But what What was there

Then he falls over And sleeps Seemingly apparently
Or is he

Unconscious
Unremembering
The memory doesn't want to be remembered
By him
And just sends its companions night sleep dream
Into Rabe's body
And they see the blood seep out of the finger joints bandaged with gauze; the white fingertips turn red, and it grows into a five finger stream, a ten finger stream, trickling and running into each other and so, while he sleeps, the flow of blood finds itself on the floor of the strange hotel room, red as a flag, red as a flame
He's not quite right in the head
Since he was down there
In the war
They always say the war is down there
Never up there or over there
Always down there

MEMOIR

A CHAIR FULL OF ASHES

Charles Harper

Of all the ways to lose a person, death is the kindest.

—Ralph Waldo Emerson

When I was six my father inherited some money. With it he bought some property and built a house. The house was made of stone and circled by forest. My father was a controlling man and used the seclusion to insulate his authority. He had the manner of a mild lunatic; I was always incurring his displeasure, which he gave me notice of by blows. My mother attempted to temper his tantrums but she was mostly silent. I walked a tightrope when he was about. The best sanctum from his ire, I found, was open space.

I spent a lot of time outdoors. I walked beneath the antique trees, their boughs woven into the lush vault of a vital cathedral. I traced rills to their springs and, taking great gulps of air, plumbed the depths of glassy ponds. In time, I knew all the land's wrinkles. But eventually the space, without anyone to fill it, became oppressive. Because of the house's remoteness, people were precious.

If I walked through the meadow, crossed the bridge, crested the hill, and plodded across the big field, I could visit my nearest neighbors. This company required a bit of labor, but because of my solitude I was willing to work.

The house was a yolk-colored rectangle anchored to a cement slab. A boy my age named Allen lived inside. Allen's family was messed up, too: His mom, Barb, was an alcoholic; she had a freeze-dried face and was all edges until she knocked a couple back. Allen's father was more rumor than reality; when he did show, usually at night, he came and went like a comet. They were poor and their house was squalid.

But Allen was a diamond in the mud. He was ambitious and eager for any enterprise. He had a crisp wit and was generous with the little he had. From

---

Charles Harper was a finalist for the 2010 PEN Prison Writing Award for Memoir.

the first symmetrical tug, we were like a binary star.

We had a common world and we explored it together. We talked of anything that came to mind, and expounded our elementary philosophies. We swam in the summer, skated in winter. We lazed days away fishing, peddled bikes over country roads. During summer we pitched camp and slept outdoors. We built bonfires in stone pits. Like two votaries we held nighttime vigils tending the flame until the last ember turned to ashes. In the dark, the world shrank to the two of us around an axis of light. With the stars wheeling overhead, we spoke and smiled.

Five years passed.

On an ordinary day when I was eleven, I walked over to Allen's house. Barb met me at the door. She was crying.

"What's wrong?"

"It's Allen... He got shot," she sobbed.

Details came out in fits and slops. Neighbor's house...kids unattended... spare bedroom...shotgun on the bed...fell, discharged.

"Is he alive?"

"He's in the hospital, in a coma."

I heard but didn't understand. After several weeks of his absence I decided to visit. I thought I could wish him well and speed his recovery. My mom drove me. We took an elevator up to a long hallway. It was silent with no activity. At the threshold a look from my mom told me I was going in alone.

The room was hot. The lights were off and the natural illumination was muted. The air was thick and smelled of unwashed body and something else. The cloying odor forced me to breathe through my mouth. Allen's unconscious body was in bed. His head was shorn; on the right side, where his eye used to be, was a metal patch. He was full of tubes; an accordion played out forced breaths with a rhythmic huff and hiss. The main wad of shot, they told me, had come out the back of his head, and they grafted a softball sized piece of bone to patch what was blown out. The quilted bone was black and looked like rotten leather. The side of his head had deep furrows. Over the wreckage, all the tender words I carried turned to chaff. I eyed the ventilator and tracked its cord into the socket... I stood there for some time, but, in the end, I failed to do or say anything.

Ten months passed. After the doctors had exhausted their arts, Allen came out of the coma and was sent home. Everyone knew he wouldn't be the same. When I saw him again up close, he was a living ruin. He was bound to a wheelchair, the cavity masked with a bad prosthesis. His head had become a piebald mosaic of plastic and flesh. The fake part had a fixed blue eye, while Allen's real eye was wild and darted like something trapped. He couldn't talk;

the noises he mouthed were all mindless. He wasn't insensate, though; judging from the moans he made he felt pain, a lot. It seemed the only thing discharged from the hospital was a hurt-stuffed husk.

I seldom visited Allen's house. When I did, I felt like I was serving a ghost. My loyalty was to the past Allen, not to this chaired Thing of the present. Allen seemed hidden, like a hard truth, behind a closed door, dirty, neglected, inconsolable. Blaming Barb would have been easy, but she did all she was capable of doing. I would have done no better, probably worse. A person in pain puts out a resonance, and I felt like a two-legged tuning fork when I was near him. The sounds he made were so forlorn, and nothing you did would soothe him. Hell is a person you can't comfort. Just a few minutes in the house would fill my mind with murk.

Barb became a fugitive from her own home. I would find her on the porch, well along in her cups. The liquor made her pain buoyant: For an instant her eyes would ignite, and everything in her seemed to float closer to the surface. Absorbed in the moment, she threw the rest of the world away. Then a low moan would issue from inside, and her face would sour.

Eight years Allen spent that way. Eight years. It was like waiting for an iceberg to melt. Before he got shot Allen weighed all of ninety pounds. Before he died he weighed close to two hundred, and whiskers were sprouting on his misshapen face like weeds in a vacant lot. When he finally died, there was no sorrow, no mourning; all these feelings had long been fossilized.

As the years pile up, by some inexplicable mental alchemy, I forget what I want to remember and remember what I want to forget. It isn't as if time has been embezzling from memory's till; rather, the chaired Thing has curdled my memory of Allen proper. It's as if someone vandalized the gallery of my memories and replaced a pedestaled masterpiece with a decomposing animal. Grappling with memory sometimes yields me a snatch of Allen's laughter, a flicker of his wit, but never his smiling face.

BLACK MIRRORS

Faraj Bayrakdar

Translated by John Asfour

This is how it is:
prison is a time
you jot down on the walls
in the early days
and in the memory
in the following months.
But when the years turn
into a long train
tired of its own whistles
and exhausted by the stations,
you try something else
similar to forgetfulness.

*

I hide
inside the poem
and look for myself outside it.
But we
conspire sometimes.
It invites me to bed
and I agree.

Faraj Bayrakdar received the Freedom to Write Award from PEN American Center in 1999. Editor of a literary journal, he was arrested in his native Syria in 1987 on political charges, held incommunicado for seven years, and subjected to torture. He was finally granted amnesty in 2000. While in prison he composed one hundred short poems, shared with other prisoners and written down with improvised ink and paper; some of these are printed here.

It takes off its clothes
and I undress.
Then, the poem wears me
yet I remain naked.

*

After one gasp
or two,
one cupful of longing
adulterated and shattered.
After beseeching one god,
a dog
or a tyrant,
my mother will enfold
fourteen skies
with my absence.

*

I am he,
I am his pronoun.
He who is absent,
who has returned from the impossible
and has gone back to it.

*

Black mirrors
are unable to see.
The white ones
do not remember.
Polished mirrors
conjure the color of detachment.
Mirror of rain,
I wish my heart were made of basalt.

*

The mirrors weep,
wipe their tears
and wrap me,
woman,
with what is not absence.

*

Four cigarettes
I would like to smoke now
all at once:
birth,
love,
freedom
and death.
Kind jailer,
let us smoke
and continue our conversation.

*

Not to be partial,
not to be boastful,
there is no other cemetery
in this life
nor in the afterlife
wider
than the one I call
my country.

*

Now I measure my age
with forty-six dances

at the edge of a precipice
and my poems do not articulate me
any more than an arrow articulates the bird
to which it sails.

*

A little while ago
I squeezed an orange
that looked like my heart.
I added a bitter alcohol
that tasted like the past
to the juice.
I took a deep breath
and lit a long thin cigarette,
its smoke resembled
the memory of a woman I never knew
then I smiled
to surprise myself.
Good evening life,
good evening friends,
good evening me.
I have invited you for the opening of the treason-teenth year
of his imprisonment.
Who of you
will cut this barbed metallic ribbon?
Do not mistake me for my grief.
I am not sad for me,
I am not sad at all.
I am only ruminating.
How plentiful are those born now
and how I wish
to toast them all
and cry
in a way
similar to longing.

FICTION

AND AND AND

Laura Lindstedt

Translated by Lola Rogers

August 6, 2000

She's drawing ampersands, &-marks on white paper, feverishly, hardly breathing. Her left hand leans against her cheek, stretching out half of her lip in a dash toward her ear, leveling out her cupid's bow, widening her nostrils. Her head has dropped its weight trustingly into her hand, but the rest of her body is rigid, tensed from the shoulders down, ready for escape.

I've tiptoed up behind her, peering over her shoulder, holding my breath. Ampersands, one after another, large ones, small ones, weak at the edges, wobbling, sometimes quick and sharp, pressing through the paper. When the A4 paper becomes too cramped, her fingers pick up a clean new sheet to put under the pencil. The smooth white paper in a diminishing pile, leaning to one side, next to it a growing stack of cellulose ornamented with ampersands, useless, covered with little black fingerprints.

The curl at the top of many of the ampersands is flattened out to a small point, which is reminiscent of the heads of prehistoric mother figurines, while the lower portion is swollen into an incredibly big ball, an overripe blister of a belly. The loop is rarely formed as an intact, unbroken coil; the pencil in its rapid circling can't find the point of intersection, instead narrowly missing it, and, annoyed at this, defying it, pulls the return point up, nearly level with the top. This gives the marks an absurd look, kicking at the air.

Now and then the beginning and end meet each other, but even then the mark doesn't resemble its uniform forefathers, who, with wise old tranquility, sit in staid forward slants, their knees briskly bent. The beginning point doesn't stand planted firmly on the ground, because the line of return tackles the character and knocks its feet out from under it, crowds too close, almost making contact with the point of departure. The loop is left to wobble, unsteady, fighting gravity. You can almost see how the conjunction is overturned, tumbling over onto its nose, turning into a brand on the flesh of a calf.

"Dear child…"

The words break off, the child's back straightens, an accusation. Her hands scoop the jumbled papers into a pile, and she squats over them protectively. I reach out a finger and try to touch her, I want to take firm hold of her, to send a message: you're safe, nothing bad has happened; I'm here, we're together now. But my hand forms a fist. One accusing finger is left standing up like it has a cramp, forces itself to creep up the child's back, causing a silent shudder. I withdraw. I gather my strength, at a loss. I try another angle of attack. I open my fist, although my fingers are against me, breath deeply, and take hold of the child's arm. I stop to listen. Nothing happens. Nothing moves. I'm starting to feel frightened. I count the seconds. Then I am rewarded: a sob.

"Show me what you've made," I request encouragingly. She lifts herself up off the papers as if she understood, hiccups tearfully, swallows and sniffles. The army of ampersands, soaked with the sweat of her fist, stands in front of us in complete disorder.

I go decisively to the dresser, dig out a pile of paper, thick, rough, yellowish. I fling them happily onto the table, stroke the top one gently like a hero returned from the war, escaped from the front, still just as beloved to a mother. Let's save those thin white ones for the printer.

I watch silently for a moment as the child warily takes a piece of paper and puts it in front of her. She rubs it between her fingers, presses it to her nose and smells. The musty air inside the box has penetrated it, and clings to the fibers. The smell wafted up to my nose, too, when I laid the pile on the table, the off-putting, cheap, porous smell of paper. I can't stay and wait. I don't want to make any apologies. I retreat back into the kitchen and let some water out into the empty sink. She'll just have to make do.

Later, I creep up to the table. She has fallen asleep with half a cheese sandwich and a glass of milk in her belly. The floorboards creak ominously under my feet. The nerve-wracking crunch follows me, increasing in strength with each step. It echoes from the walls and ceiling like a smothered giggle, rebounding from the corners and carpets like suppressed laughter, becoming a mocking screech in my ears. The scratch paper hasn't been touched. The thick sheets are in a neat pile at the edge of the table, just as I left them. Instead, the messy ampersands have been taken up again, the paper turned sideways. Because of the numerous additional strokes and the abundant coloring, I can't seem to recognize the previous clusters of conjunctions, which have now become schools of a million fish. They swim away, as long as me, scatter in their own directions as if they've spotted a predator.

It ripened in me surreptitiously, only half noticed, somehow, one autumn, and everything started to appear in a new light: what if there were two plates there, and what if there were two drinking glasses, too. There on my kitchen table. I couldn't yet see the rest back then—I was living in a studio apartment, with a separate, small kitchen, and there was an alcove, a queen-sized bed behind a reed mat, enough room for me. And then it started to become crowded. In my mind. Three years back—with two each of plates, glasses, forks, knives, and spoons. A small bed started to form in the corner, too, and a child's voice, a little girl's beckoning whispers, the hollow pressed by a kiss into the cheek. That's when I knew to make a couple of phone calls.

Things were set in motion quickly. They took me seriously right from the start—the officials. They mailed heaps of papers for me to read—diagrams, statistics, contact information. I didn't breathe a word to anyone else, not yet. I was burying my thoughts, keeping them quite to myself, letting my studio fill up and fill up, letting myself be silly, letting my feet pull me along. I found myself in the children's section of a department store, surrounded by children's clothing, holding a three-year-old's light blue sweater in my hands—and I put it away, quickly. It was too small in my hands. It was an incomprehensibly small knitted thing, almost doll clothing, made of soft alpaca yarn, knit, purl, knit, purl. I folded the sweater and put it back on the shelf and continued my journey, away from the rompers, with snaps that reached from the neck opening all the way to the heels. It would be easy to slide a child into them, a little thing kicking the air might even slip in there by itself, a little foot like a delectable sausage sliding into the pants, safely in with one kick, one skillfully intercepted kick into place, then the toes would be properly in, well inside the foot. And then the fists, flailing at emptiness, too, and the dirty diapers to dig out from inside the romper and all of that everyday stuff to do again: the teeny tiny bottom washed under the water, the fingernails emasculated with the clippers. Then finally a fingerful of ointment, and another, every single day. No—not too small a child for me!

I found a six-inch toy giraffe in the toy department, and for some reason I bought it. *Would you like a bag, or shall I perhaps wrap it up*, the young suck-up said, with his whiskers like fluff, obviously never went to school, since there were only two flags on his badge for the languages he spoke: Finland's and Britain's. No, just like this is fine, on the bottom of my bag, right in there, and thanks, no bag: I don't use plastic bags. I prefer not to. I already have too many at home. On the top shelf in the entryway closet, and if the door comes open... they tumble out! I can't fit any more inside, there's not the smallest bit of space left! No bag for me, thanks.

When I got home I stood the giraffe on top of the television, a gray and white 28-inch mass that was much too large for the apartment, and had the distinction of being the one expensive corner of my home. I regretted the purchase for a long time—yes, it was a mistake. I felt half obliged to buy it from the man who sold it to me, smiling: a new era was beginning, a digital era, you'll be ready for this new era if you buy now, a widescreen television at half price! High definition technology, it's waiting in our future. Think about it—if you buy now, you've already got the equipment! He slapped the console with his hand, walked around it, and looked at me again, smiling and staring straight into my eyes, a crazy man who kept talking, always talking.

So there they were: the squashed faces, pudgy trees, stretched houses. I couldn't find the right settings, the manual was stupid, full of writing errors—*ideal picture settings values recording*—good God! Never mind. The picture size had to be reset every time you turned it on, and I gave up and got used to it. I only reset it last Christmas, for *Fanny and Alexander*. Those wonderful table settings! Room after room, satin, porcelain! And the people: the adults, those idiots, those artfully-built puppets whose existence the old master had locked up in a few lines of dialogue, virtuous, chuckling, over-confident: he was this sort of man, she was that sort of woman, can you believe it? One absent-minded gesture, one stray look, and that's the kind of man he is, can you believe that? It was a movie I loved to hate. I loved the pig's head, the candles, the crystal chandeliers. I hated the characters—all of them except for Fanny and Alexander. The giraffe looked at me from under his long, curled eyelashes, and I ate rutabaga casserole. I pressed the plus button for more volume whenever the music played, and got myself some more beet salad. I fetched some more liver casserole and glazier's herring, ate myself sick, almost unconscious. I had made every traditional Christmas dish myself from start to finish. I wanted to practice a little, and I didn't have a proper freezer at the time: I ate it all. I ate and rested, ate and rested. I watched television and turned it off, blew out the candles, and rested. I breathed in the scent of hyacinths, carnations, pepper, paraffin, and it was wonderful, in spite of all the pain and constipation and queasiness. It may have even been too wonderful: my best Christmas ever.

Of course, I really had a reason to celebrate, because they had found a child for me in China! It happened fast, it only took about six months. *They named a child unusually quickly*, the agent in Finland rejoiced, *You got lucky*. Things were churning around in Finland for about a year—first me, then the papers. Now it was over. Now I just had to agree to the proposition and wait to be invited on a journey.

So break out the champagne! I brought a bottle of Taittinger to work first thing on Monday. The progress of the whole affair had been closely watched for half a year. It was no longer a secret—no, it was a general subject of conversation, perhaps even tiresome already. At the beginning of every week they asked *How's it going?* patted me on the back, *Anything happening yet? Has the ball started rolling?* and one of them, the one unhappy soul who was like a broken record the whole fall: *Any news? Any news?* Quite out of breath, in an abrasive voice, breaking after the climb up the stairs, drooling in the doorway: *Any n-news y-yet?* Water on the tongue. Beads of sweat on the bridge of her nose. And she smelled: Fii brand roll-on and a musty attic. Phew! Damn. Underarms fertilized with bacterial growth—doesn't she realize? She could wash her clothes in vinegar, or better yet buy some new ones! *Any news? Anything?*

It gradually started to grow tiresome: always the same answer, in the same purring voice: waiting, just waiting now.

After Christmas, I didn't have to wait much longer. We had four more days on watch, and we all clinked delicate crystal goblets, which were a long-ago bribe from the Soviet Union. How do you solve problems with them where you work, if they come up? In our office we believe that quarrels between comrades can be solved without taking anyone to court! We have a proper vodka delegation, a week's trip to get to know each other, hot saunas every night, and they bring us glasses, and take home stockings for their wives as souvenirs. And shoes! Black, white, yellow, leather shoes, silk shoes, suede shoes—and perfumes—and handbags! Antelope skin, chamois, silk! Our older colleagues always laughed about that trip when they clinked their goblets. But they weren't there anymore, they were with their families, their grandchildren, at home. The four of us gave a toast in the fluorescent light of the break room. The new millennium would begin on Saturday. To a new era and a new mother, a good reason to toast, indeed. *A thousand happinesses!*

August 10, 2000

And. And. And. I'm trying to fish out a meal from around that empty word. I'm making her some food, asking her what she would like. Fish sticks and? Hot dogs and? She doesn't react although I lower the difficulty level by switching to treats. Strawberries and? Animal crackers and? The pieces don't fit into place, and it seems that she's not even trying. She stares at me with her slanted eyes, lets her head fall a little, doesn't even utter half a syllable. No smile, no wrinkled brow, just a look, and yet not seeing me.

We started practicing as soon as she had been here a few days, at the end of Easter week, on a trip to the store. I'd run out of something—milk of course, and coffee—everybody was coming by to have a cup. They came in little clusters, gushing in the door, everyone bringing something, wondering at how little she was, and pretty, she was going to be a pretty girl some day. And then we ran out of milk.

I dressed her in a red snowsuit, put wool mittens on her hands, a wool scarf around her neck, sheepskin shoes on her feet, size twenty-six. April was cold, there was black snow along the roads and a cold wind that went right through you: the pine trees trembled outside the window, their tops bending, their clusters of branches curtseying humbly, standing up, then curtseying again, rising and falling as if on springs. I pulled the zipper closed, right to the top. The little bakelite clasps disappeared into the jaws of the slider, melted together inside it, scrunched tightly into each others' gaps, and then the snowsuit was on.

We stepped into the elevator, right to the back of it. The mirror was covered, broken, someone had come in too fast and crashed their head against it during the night: I'd heard the noise, the splitting glass, the shout, and now a covered-up place where the mirror was. I pulled the child closer, held onto her hood—no, don't touch anything, keep your hands and feet still. Look—the floors passing by, the numbers changing: five, four, three, two, one, ground floor: this is where we get off, where we go outside.

We went outside for the first time together. We crossed the parking lot, walked along the path, under the bridge, into the mega shopping center. We went from baked goods to fruit, fruit to dairy, dairy to meat, and finally to the freezer section. People looked at us. Heads turned, the wheels of the shopping carts stopped grating along the linoleum floor for a moment, then started moving again, as soon as I raised my eyes, the wheels rattled again, people hurried to the steaming frozen foods bins, peas corn peppers, the wheels rattling away, and the two of us were alone again.

The child sat quietly in the cart and I babbled breakfast at her: cereal, bananas, yogurt. I chattered about lunch, pea soup, and fish sticks for dinner. I also put two liters of the red milk in the cart, for coffee, in case someone else comes over. In case someone pops in to visit, chirping with their syrupy grins, what a pretty girl. Thin as can be, small, but she'll plump up all right. Cram some butter on everything she eats, pour a little cream in it, she'll develop right before your eyes.

That's still a goal of mine, to get her weight up. I set the table brimful, get the jars out of the fridge five times a day. I surround the child with little cups filled with tomatoes and pickles. The yellow pickles wait with their forks upraised in a blue cup, the slices of beet overlap flirtatiously at the bottom of a green dish. I set slices of rye fanning out upright on the bread platter, with a battalion of oven-fresh rolls, cut in half, arranged below them.

Scaleless right-angled pieces of cod dive onto a plate between cartons of milk and piimä. The golden yellow, breaded fillets cling to each other as the pieces of fish swim circles in their cramped pool. They finally tire and are left dozing in the shade of an outcropping of mashed potatoes. I herd the school of cod into the compost container in the evening, on top of the dried-up bread and shriveled vegetables.

The next time I try to be more crafty. I chop the frankfurters into a laugh, sink lingonberry eyes into the cabbage rolls. I send a strawberry to climb the outcrop of whipped cream, conjure up animal crackers in a circle around the Sun Jaffa glass. I dig out the narrow blue linen table runner stashed in the cabinet and plop it down as a fjord in the centre of the table. I arrange three ramekins of dipping sauce on the narrow stripes of the fabric: I slip a provision of fresh dill into one, crumble salty Aura cheese into the second, and try some hot paprika in the third. Last of all, I stand potato chip sails in them and wait for the regatta to begin. In vain.

Nothing tastes good, nothing will do. She messes the food up putting it on her plate, unrolls the cabbage leaves, skins the laughs off the frankfurters. She puts out her tongue and licks the whipped cream, licks the ballet dancer off of the back of her pink cookie. She pushes a finger into the spicy sour cream, sucks on it, and makes a face. She only bothers to drink half a glass of the bubbly lemonade, and doesn't ask for more of anything.

Every evening before the news, I carry her away and put her under the blanket. After a goodnight kiss, I go back and sit on the sofa. I don't watch the television, on mute, the news anchors opening their mouths, don't pay any attention to the cleanup after the bombing in a pedestrian tunnel in downtown Moscow, or the stiff pantomime of the militias, or the silent statement of the mayor. I'm listening. My lips itch, something moves into my bloodstream along with my saliva. The itch sinks down my throat, pricks my esophagus, presses as far as my stomach, murmuring. Then it's silent.

There was hardly ever any noise at all. A stumble, a rustling, my voice. For the first couple of days, I enjoyed it for a little while—a new kind of vibration in my throat. A voice not charged up for a meeting—that slightly pompous, sometimes skittish and shrill, sometimes even twittering meeting voice. It's amazing what it can accomplish sometimes—mouse-quiet, harmlessly cooing, or with a reckless, irritated guffaw that ends as if at a wall, and then it's back to business. It's like surreptitiously tightening a loose screw, no one notices it.

To my child I spoke in uncomplicated language. My voice latched onto anything at all that was around me, my mouth spit out whatever it could manage to grasp, willy-nilly. This little spoon here, we should wash it, that cloth there over the cupboard door, let's dry the spoon with it. There's the slam of the mail slot, the day's mail, advertisements, let's pick them up off the floor. These papers, let's put them in the recycling, those curtains, closed: it's already dark, they'll see inside from the house across the street, it's time to close the curtains!

Then it started to be troubling. A narrator in my apartment. It started to sound bizarre: like a blabbermouth, and much too strict. The place was cleaner than ever before, clean from top to bottom, needless things were taken to the attic, even more needless ones to the cellar, useful ones stayed on this floor, new things were brought from the furniture store in a delivery truck. But something started to constrict, and I started to get a bad feeling, to feel dizzy, to want to vomit. I usually stopped chatting around six o'clock. I drank some water, from a liter bottle. My throat hurt, my voice was hoarse: it didn't sound like me any more. It was best not to waste my strength—but it was about time the girl got used to the language!

She fit herself into the apartment quickly, started to move through the rooms like she was at home. She would get up from the table just like that, in the middle of everything, and sneak into the other room. I often followed after her. I skittered after her like a dustbunny, veered off on my own course before she could turn around. Sometimes I was there to meet her. I would sit in a chair, open my arms, scoop up the air in a relaxed manner, and she would come along with it. She fixed her eyes on me, sat in my lap, and I put a light kiss on her cheek with a smack. Sometimes it worked, usually it didn't. There were torturous moments, a small underlying tremble that you could feel in both of us, a limp jerk that struck us together at the wrong places: shoulders, knees, round-edged overhangs. Then embarrassment, having to get away: off you go, now, let's make a sandwich.

And we made a sandwich, put gobs of butter on it, a slice of ham, and a plate underneath. So there she sat crumbling it as I thought of my next move.

I ran out of ideas quickly. Ideas for things to do. The food was a mess, the picture books looked through. Then the day was over, just like always—the child lay under the blanket in the dark, and I sat on the sofa. I sank deeper into the leather folds of the couch, sinking toward the springs, nearer to the treacherous trap of metal coils. I listened, I waited for drowsiness—if I could get up the courage to go to bed myself soon. It's peculiar to be in there, in the same darkness with her. Right next to her, near the little pull-out bed. It would be easy to reach out my hand from my own bed. It could lightly brush her hair, as if by accident, in the middle of a dream, if a dream caused a large movement of the hand, then it would be there. In her hair. Maybe the bed should be moved a little, a half a meter, maybe her breathing wouldn't bother me then, a quick, slightly tugging snuffle deep in my ears, a troubling tug that catches below my long breaths. Is she not getting enough oxygen? When I creep into the bedroom at night, the air is thick with carbon dioxide. I open the window, let in some fresh night air, a new moon, wind spiced with evergreen. It doesn't help much—the air is still heavy, breathing is laborious somehow, and that is such a disagreeable sensation: the feeling of breathing. The feeling of pulling air inside—you start to observe it. You start to count the breaths without realizing it: Will it keep going? Will your own chest rise? Quite by itself it rises, regardless of what I do, doesn't it? It's impossible to sleep in there now!

But she sleeps, and gets up. Every morning, at seven o'clock to the minute, she comes and pokes me in the side with a finger. She always needs something, otherwise she would sleep forever. I have to guess what it is. I get out of bed and feel her feet. Is it a cold morning? Should we look for some slippers? If I miss the mark, she withdraws a couple of steps backward and looks at me amazed.

The white sheet has been crumpled beneath me during the night, the landing strip is blistered with treacherous little waves. But the blanket is still lifted invitingly. It hasn't fled onto the floor in the wee hours, it hasn't escaped in a twisted bundle at the foot of the bed. It is waiting for the little traveller, promising shelter, pledging ready warmth.

I want to sink my child into that warmth completely. I would start with her legs, enfold them in a cocoon of blanket, tuck the quilt under her heels. I would insulate her skin carefully, not leaving a single opening for the air to get in. I would press the blanket tightly against her skin, seal up her skinny sides, her narrow arms and slender neck. And then her little kisser, and shnozzola, and peepers! Her whole little self, the whole kit and caboodle, all wrapped up. Where did she go?!

I start to poke my fingers into her armpits, infiltrate them under her arms, which are pressed down at her sides, careful not to scrape her delicate skin. Her linen shirt chafes my fingers. The eclipsed half moons of cuticle screech against the linen, leathery slivers of skin poke out and catch on the fibers. When the fingers are finally in place, I grab her chest with my thumbs and lift. She's as heavy as lead. Her small arms slip unnaturally as I struggle to press her into the air.

I quickly foist her onto the edge of the bed. I fetch some wool socks from the wardrobe, thread them onto her frozen feet, put some leggings on her, too, to hold the saggy cuffs of her socks up. When the strip of skin around her ankles is finally covered in wool, I lift her back onto the floor and we walk together toward the living room.

The pattern of steps is familiar, well-trodden. We always circle back into the living room by way of the toilet. I sit on the big pot, she on the little plastic one. Then we wait, careful not to look each other in the eye. We subside into our own thoughts. Or maybe it's a race to see who'll finish first. I'm much too tense to be able to take care of my own job—I'm concentrating on listening. Concentrating on her look of concentration. She strokes the edges of the potty absent-mindedly, picks up the fringe on the plastic bath mat with her toes.

I'm not a criminal. They wanted to know that, too: that I'm not a criminal. I ordered a criminal registry report from the central judicial register as soon as my contract with the agency was confirmed. The report had to be requested in writing, and it came in a week, from Hämeenlinna. The upper and lower margins were emblazoned in violet, and it wasn't an accident, that beautiful, startling purple: sackcloth and ashes! That's what it meant. A cross from a priestly finger in the middle of the forehead: accept the mark of penitence! That's exactly what it meant. There's nothing in these letters for purely aesthetic reasons—the colors, the fonts, the line spacing, all of it is carefully thought out, burnished with an ancient liturgy: hints no one notices that nevertheless start to secretly haunt the hiding places in the furrows of your brain, to get you to quiet down, think about fasts, lentil soup and water, reform, a change of direction. Goodbye meat! No, it's not an accident, they know precisely what color paper to use.

I didn't have any marks on my record. *Am Tag der Ausgabe dieses Auszugs gibt es über die obengenannte Person keine Eintragungen im Strafregister Finnlands.* It was written in four different languages: No recorded crimes. A certified good girl.

These are serious matters. Supremely serious matters, and you shouldn't play around with them. It's inappropriate, this is about your life, many people's lives, and dreams—and dreams are sacred. They may even be everlasting. They live a lot longer than we do: qualified to be a mother, designated to be a daughter—they remain in office files, in institutional desk drawers, agency binders. It's a relief, actually: everything's filed, trails we've left behind us, that the child has left behind without knowing it—of course she doesn't know it. She just happened to be born, given away, happened to continue breathing, tugging oxygen in like a little machine, blowing air out like a tiny little engine, like a device preset to repeat itself, once it's gone through one cycle, the contraption never stops working again! It's baffling: even when you throw it away, the dang thing doesn't stop living. On the contrary: when you throw it away it clings to life tighter than ever! The best of these, the fortunate ones, they rattle into a new place like grains in a silo. The straw, chaff, and weed seeds drop out of the works, oops, they disappear, grow into children you won't find in the statistics but in the factories and cart shafts and streets: glue, solvent, lacquer, butane, straight in with the rhythm of each breath, from crumpled plastic bags! And look: everything is beautiful for a moment: like the colors on the surface of an oil slick, like fractal flowers germinating in the concrete.

But the best ones, the luckiest babies, who continue the journey, have heavier burdens than the ones left along the way. Like boulders! They throw themselves forward along the conveyor belt, dash through the powerful blast of the winnowing fan: they are fed, and they drink, and sleep, sleep, sleep like princesses, and then, one beautiful day, some of them notice: I'm still here. When they're two years old they finally notice that five-kilo babies are leaving all around them. At three years old they notice that the teeny tiny arrivals just vanish like that. At four years old, they notice that the very small bundles, still suckling, are snatched away to someplace, up, into someone's arms, white arms, sometimes brown arms in the summer, because some of us have the habit of tanning in the summer, some of us enjoy the outdoor life, pulling weeds and lying on the boulders at the beach, some of us read thrillers in a hammock. Because that's just the way it is: in the summer you have permission to get off on crime. *Here's the Knutssons' phone number. They're expecting your call!* Some of them have already flown a long way to a strange country, a country they've never been to before, a country they've been dreaming about for a long time— there, that's where we'll go, as soon as we get word. Everything's ready: two weeks' worth of clothes, gifts wrapped in rustling paper, a comfortable high-rise apartment in Kulosaari. Because they'll get one from somewhere, if not from the stork. A little bundle. If you wish hard enough you'll get your wish—and they look at each other with faint happiness. The woman and the man. They've left a considerable trail, they've produced piles of paperwork, court cases. *Only a crazy person—or a lawyer!—can survive this mess.* They smile: that's how much they love this little one.

The man takes a little girl who's just learned to walk in his arms. A girl. Of course it's a girl, only girls come from that country—black-haired, sloe-eyed darlings, sent on their way by an accident, or to be on the safe side—you never know if you might get a boy, if fortune favors you. For that you'd even give up your tax break. But not for a girl, girls are nothing but a nuisance. *A little nuisance,* that's what they say to me in their spacious Biedermeier living room, *what a lovely little nuisance,* their very own nuisance! They sink into the soft backs of their walnut veneer chairs at almost the same time.

They babble and laugh, a piercingly clear laugh, a bellow that goes through everything, a post-fertility treatment laugh, a laugh smoothed from years of waiting, the laugh of peers, rounded by too many disappointments, and they assure me: you'll be one of us next year, for sure.

They tell me about their experiences, their feelings, *this might be helpful to you,* to make it easier to orient yourself. To imagine. Then later, when the child has been brought home, we'll get together for a barbecue. And outings, lazy rambles, camping at the edge of the wilderness. You're always welcome! Family activities: men and women and children. Women and children. Children and women. Men and women. Children and children. A sea of children. Voices. The murmur of voices. Hustle and bustle. And me and the child, too—us, too, certainly. Next year then.

August 12, 2000

Scissors. Now she's found the scissors.

She went into the kitchen, and I want to know what she's up to in there. I wait quietly in the hallway, from there I can see everything except the counter around the corner. She's bustling around, looking first at the things at eye level. Cupboards whose contents she must have investigated many times already, handles that you can pull on to get to the pots, pans, forks, knives, dry goods, garbage bags, potting soil. She raises her eyes and notices something hanging on a nail about a meter and sixty centimeters up. The orange-handled Fiskars and a large soup ladle dangle from the rack next to the twine, a hot pad separated from its mate, and a dirty dishtowel.

She stands with her shoulders hunched up and stares. She fetches the wooden stool, positions it under the rack, and climbs up onto it.

She can just barely reach the scissors. She takes them off the hook with a grunt and stares at them for a moment triumphantly. Like an ape who has through her own ingenuity got possession of the bunch of bananas hanging from the ceiling, not realizing that her efforts are being monitored. Then comes the difficult descent. She tries to get down on her knees onto the top of the stool. She holds the sharp, dangerous weapon in one hand, groping at the wall for support with the other. I close my eyes. Wait for her to crash to the floor in a heap, with the blade of the scissors shoved through her heart. Eyes rolling around and a flash of red mouth, open, limp. Harakiri? No. A child murdered!

No.

An accident.

Just a scratch.

Just a little scrape!

She'll be fine, if she has an accident. You just wet a cotton ball with disinfectant, dab it on the cut, squeeze a little liquid on the gash. The bacteria will foam under the little flap of skin, hissing and seething and finally dying off. You cut a strip of bandage to the right size, a centimeter or two, press a cushion of gauze carefully over the wound. Pull away protective papers, press the adhesive surface lightly against the skin. It can breathe in there, through the little holes. It won't stew in there or get wet, but breathe. Heal over. Get better. Just like that, all by itself!

Everybody gets hurt when they're little. When they don't yet know the strength of their own limbs, the exact length of their extremities, the tiny difference between the edge and emptiness. Oh, the confidence with which they put the bottom of their foot down! Not a trace of worry, even if only the heel lands on the top of the stool, the slippery sock sliding over the surface, the toes and the ball of the foot with nothing under them. No, not the smallest doubt that there's enough room on the half-circle of stool for a knee, even though the other foot totters firmly in the middle, without moving a centimeter, not giving an inch.

Then the crying, face twisted into a pout, lower lip starting to tremble. I would pick her up in my arms, the poor little thing, from where she fell, next to the stool. I would pick up the scissors from the rug, put them back up on the rack: No! Those aren't for kids to play with!

I hear a sniff and the rustle of clothing, a little knocking as the leg of the stool lifts unsteadily into the air when the weight is thrown off balance, and hits the floor again as the weight shifts. Then it's quiet. I open my eyes. She's standing firmly in one piece, glancing around with a guilty look. I quickly withdraw deeper into the darkness of the hallway. She places the scissors on the table, puts the stool back where she got it and grabs the scissors again.

She takes hold of the scissors clumsily, turns them in her hands. Lifts them to eye level and peeps through the openings. Then she puts her tongue in the thumb opening and starts to lick the plastic. Her tongue circles the edge ardently, pressed against the plastic as if glued there by centrifugal force. Now and then the whole thumb piece disappears into her pouting mouth as she slurps up the spit and sucks the slippery circle dry.

Then she holds onto the blade and puts the handles between her knobby little knees, squeezed against her pants. She pushes the scissors back and forth, trying to dry the inner surface against the hemisphere of her knee. When that job is done, she picks them up in her hand again.

All four of her fingers fit through the handle. Her thumb is bent around the round opening, her nails turn white from the force of her grasp. Then the clacking starts. Open, closed, open, closed. The scissors cut the air into different sized slices, careless shreds. I see her in profile, turning quietly ninety degrees, toward the kitchen door. The blades point at me. She walks forward in time with the clacking, the scissors like an icebreaker. I escape on tiptoe into the small neighboring room, the play room, with teddy bear wallpaper that I put up myself. I stumble over a railroad track, but find a place to put my foot at the last minute, between the train station and the pasture, ten centimeters from the Brio tower. I listen for where the clacking ended up. At first it feels like the scissors are approaching me. Then the sound gets weaker, and finally goes completely silent. I gather my courage and peek out the door.

GEOGRAPHIES OF THE POSSIBLE

ALBERT MOBILIO: Utopia and dystopia seem to constitute certain geographies of the possible. The word utopia, of course, in the Greek means "no place," but there have been many attempts to realize utopias. The last century certainly saw its share, and in the present century we see fundamentalist religious groups of all stripes working toward their versions of utopia, whether it be the rapture or the caliphate. But the key word, I think, for our discussion is "possibility." Does literature create possibilities—social, psychological, interpersonal, material possibilities? And just how does this happen? And is this notion of creating possibility through your work something that you actively seek—or perhaps something that you avoid?

JONATHAN LETHEM: I always felt a very active engagement with the notions of utopia and dystopia, partly because I grew up as a reader inside the subculture of science fiction, where those ideas are taken as commonplaces. Of course, in the larger world of politics or culture, they're quite troublesome words, but in science fiction they simply name bunches of books. So the idea that you might be attracted to one or the other mode was something I auditioned in a fairly unassuming way. It didn't bear an enormous freight of responsibility—it was more a matter of my appetite for stories. I thought, "Well, I like George Orwell and Philip K. Dick. I must be one of those 'dystopian' people."

And I do see my work in terms of framing possibilities, but in an even more fundamental sense. The act of asserting the possibility of another world—to be auditioned, let alone desired—is very much at stake, I think, both in literary and political culture right now. Because we live in a time when there is a denial of utopian envisioning as a legitimate frame of reference. Slavoj Žižek has a notorious remark: He says it's actually easier to get people into a conversation about a meteor travelling through space and hitting the earth and ending all life as we know it than to get people into a serious conversation about the end of the liberal capitalist consensus. In other words, it's much easier to consider life ending on

---

This transcript was adapted from a conversation that took place at the 2010 PEN World Voices Festival. Inga Kuznetsova's Russian was interpreted by Laura Wolfson; Andrzej Stasiuk's Polish was interpreted by Eva Sadowska.

the planet than to consider a political framework different from the one we have accepted as the inevitable compromised ideal towards which we're all trudging in a kind of fatal consensus. And I think the fundamental act, the primal act, of literary imagination is to immerse a single individual in the possibility of another consciousness. So simply by reading a novel or poem we're accepting the possibility of a mind outside of our own. And literature asserts not just the possibility but the *value* of exploring another subjectivity—which I think is analogous to the crucial, fragile possibility that it could be valuable from within this fatal consensus to visualize some other form of social organization in our world.

MOBILIO: This imagining of some other form of social organization—does it carry risk? Here on the stage we have writers from Russia, Poland, Israel—and Jonathan from the United States, a country with its own messianic pretensions. We just had a century marked by nationalist efforts to reorganize society along utopian lines and, in some of those cases at least, there was dystopian fallout. I wonder, Andrzej, is this something you think about in your own work, that the imagining of possible social alternatives might somehow implicate the writer?

ANDRZEJ STASIUK: It's difficult to say. I lived for thirty years in a utopian system, and mostly it was just very boring. I'm quite satisfied with what's around me now. I create a literary utopia, but a very private, very intimate utopia that I create for my own purposes. I am not trying to create a new world that would demonstrate a different form of social organization. I take the world, I cut it into small pieces, and I glue it together again, and this is my story—this is what I like about the world, and this is what I like about my literary work.

MOBILIO: I read that as a young man you left the Polish army—or, perhaps, deserted the Polish army—and then joined a pacifist organization. Perhaps in your own life, or in your life as a citizen, you allow yourself utopian goals—but not in your fiction?

STASIUK: It's true that I deserted the army, but not because I was a pacifist. I did it because the army was very boring. And many of my friends who were active in the pacifist movement decided that I was a very precious person, and they helped me, so maybe that's where that story comes from. I'm ashamed to admit it, but I liked the army. I imagine if there were a war maybe I would have stayed. But unfortunately there was no war at that time.

MOBILIO: A war probably would not be boring.

STASIUK: War wouldn't have been boring, that's for sure. I think what's behind those apparently pacifistic or utopian gestures is simply boredom.

MOBILIO: Perhaps that's what's behind the creation of all art.

STASIUK: I think that's true. Art and literature might be an answer to the boredom of life.

MOBILIO: Inga, you also hail from a former Communist country, one of the great utopias of the twentieth century. How did that affect your decision to become a poet and how does it affect your poetry?

INGA KUZNETSOVA: Life in a self-styled attempt at utopia probably forced me to distance myself from an aggressive political stance. It's my opinion that the existence of a state lowers, or even denigrates, people, because the purpose of a state or government is to bring together many different interests and achieve a common denominator—but human beings are much bigger than that. They exist between heaven and earth, and literature is the only area where there is true utopia that brings it all together. Thank God our government no longer interferes in the creation of art. There were superb poets who could not publish unless they attached themselves to a literary magazine as a sort of caboose—the only way they could get published is if they wrote a text that exalted the Communist Party and the government. That text served to carry them and their real work through to the public, like the front car that pulls the train behind it and brings it into the platform. If there wasn't such a text attached to a work, a book might, at the last minute, not make it into print or might be very severely cut.

For a long time we had the tradition of writing for the desk drawer—you knew what you wrote was not going to be published. I believe the situation was similar in Poland. During the height of totalitarianism—and by that I mean the Stalin years—classic Russian literature and classical music were like an oasis where people could flee from time to time to have a genuine sense of being alive. It's my feeling that the greater the distance between the state and the creative writer, the better that is for literature—and the better it is if there's less assistance of a material nature as well. I believe that poetry is utopia, and that both readers and writers, when they are immersed in poetry, are in paradise.

MOBILIO: Perhaps utopia exists in language, in the space between the reader's eyes and the page. On the other hand, one of the last century's utopian visions was the Zionist vision, which is very much about a particular plot of earth. Eshkol, in your most recent novel, *Homesick*, you write about a contested home and a contested place. The notion of home and the notion of utopia—are these both, in some way, unachievable phantoms?

ESHKOL NEVO: As an Israeli you can't underestimate the power of utopian literature. Theodor Herzl wrote *Altneuland*, or *Old New Land*, more than one hundred years ago. When the book came out, he was ridiculed in his own country by critics and by readers. And by the way, when you read this book with the eyes of today, as a literary creation, it has its problems. Sometimes I imagine a student bringing *Altneuland* to my writing workshop, and I examine it with literary eyes. The characters are too predictable, the narrative is not so good...

Jonathan mentioned science fiction. It was science fiction to imagine a land, a territory, for the Jews—and sixty years afterwards it became reality. Now, while becoming reality, while realizing this dream, this utopia, it became a dystopia for another nation, the Palestinians. The 1948 war was the realization of the utopia, and the creation of a dystopia for another nation. So in my book *Homesick* there are different kinds of longings, different homes and homesicknesses. It takes place in a little town called Mevasseret. While I was researching the book, I found out that this Jewish town is situated on the ruins of a Palestinian village, so, I thought, "How can I write a book about homesickness without writing about people who are living there?" This was their home. What happens when a utopia of one nation meets a dystopia of another nation? In my book, I make it very practical, so to speak. An Arab construction worker working in a Jewish neighborhood begins to suspect that the house in front of him is the house where he was born and raised. So he goes to his mother and asks her about it. She says, "Go and check, and bring me something from the house. I forgot something behind in the war"—the War of Independence, as it is called by Israelis, and the Nakba, as it is called by the Palestinians. This Arab construction worker, in a moment that is a junction of utopia and dystopia, enters the house, wanting something back from his childhood. Utopia and dystopia meet in Israel on a daily basis, I think.

LETHEM: There's a striking thing that American identity and Israeli identity have in common: We live in the only two countries I can think of that are basically science fiction novels, or conceptual projects. You know, manifest destiny is a concept—the westward expansion, the acquisition of most of our territory, the forging of the railway link: These are conceptual projects. We don't have one founding novel as our origin story, but the countries are both conceptual projects laid over the grounds of the civilizations that happened to be in place when we arrived.

But I'm very conscious of also being, in a funny way, the representative here of a rare species: someone who came of age in a more or less conscious dystopia.

In New York in the 1970s—the early part of the '70s in particular—people were free to declare their disappointment with the collapse of the project. There was mercifully no political suppression of discontent. I thought of this today, realizing how the subways are sort of grinding towards ruin again—they're canceling lines, and it's reminding me a little bit of 1973. This was then a consciously fallen place. New York had been great and had collapsed, and everyone felt that way about it. If you look at the art and the popular narratives that emerged from New York City in that period—*Death Wish* and *The French Connection* and Paula Fox's *Desperate Characters*; or, to take it back to science fiction, Samuel Delany's great novel *Dhalgren*—they're about people who know they're living in ruins. There's the famous Gerald Ford swipe at Abe Beame's bankrupt New York City: "Drop dead." Well, many people felt we were living in a corpse of greatness—that sane people had fled, and the ones left were living in a squalid dystopia.

Which, paradoxically, was exhilarating, and became an opportunity. You encounter this in a portrayal like Delany's *Dhalgren*: It became a utopia by default, a place—because power had abandoned it and privilege was receding in favor of a kind of anarchist, artistic, blank canvas—where anything could be created. And it was terrifying and thrilling at the same time. That's not to claim any special trauma; I still was fundamentally living in what used to be called the First World, before the Second World disappeared. But there was a narrative quite different from the concept of westward expansion and the culmination of an American utopia. It had failed. Watergate and so on—that was the era I came of age within: "Oh, too bad, the story didn't work. Now what?"

NEVO: It's fascinating how all of this was happening here, in the United States. For many Israelis, in the same years you're talking about—the '70s and '80s—the American dream was our utopia. I think the Jewish people have been split in half. In the '40s and '50s, half of them went to live in Israel and create this utopia, and the other half went to the United States, more or less. So, since then, this is our *other* possibility—the road not taken for Israelis is the American dream. So, just when it was deteriorating, as you were feeling it, for the Israelis it was a dream.

LETHEM: I can't hear this without thinking of Philip Roth's *Operation Shylock*, where, in typical Rothian agony, he thinks again and again how simple it would have been to carve out a more or less Israel-sized chunk of Montana, or something, and just hand it over, and never have your story go in this horrible direction.

MOBILIO: Your new novel *Chronic City*, Jonathan, represents a New York where maximum possibility and maximum despair often exist in the same locale, simultaneously. Andrzej, your novel *Nine* portrays a kind of post-Communist, post-dystopia Poland—but no one's very happy. Jonathan describes authority receding from New York and leaving a more open, freer city, one that produces an explosion, perhaps, of artistic energy. But the world you depict in your novel is a very unhappy place, even with the absence of Communist tyranny.

STASIUK: There are many people in Poland who are still unhappy because Communism has passed. But my book *Nine* is not about Communism; it is not a political book. It is more a book about loneliness, about a life that's been untangled, and different coincidences and different serendipities. People in this book are unhappy because *people* are unhappy. I think, after having spent three days in New York, I could write a very similar book about New York.

MOBILIO: There's plenty of unhappiness here. It's our chief export, I think. And those are the existential verities: how each individual relates to and somehow exists within a larger political sphere. Perhaps our metaphysical poet might have something to say about how those existential issues relate to various forms of social organization.

KUZNETSOVA: In the brief period that I've been in the United States, from what I've been able to learn, American poets work thanks to the concern and care extended to them by the government. Whereas Russian poets do their work despite an absence of the same. Or maybe it's not the government or the state, but just the conditions here—I mean, it's so pleasant and so warm… unfortunately, I haven't written anything while I've been here. I did a bit of shopping. In Russia, it's much easier to write about the most exalted things— the metaphysical and the highest things in life, the essence of life—precisely because physical existence is more problematic. Maybe I'm exaggerating a bit. Last year, I went through a period where I felt the things we were writing, my friends and I—and the situation with poetry is really quite favorable in Russia right now—that what we were writing wasn't really needed or of interest to a larger audience. And, when I go to poetry readings, either to read my own work or to hear my friends read, it's always the same people in the audience: poets, writers, and critics. Well, not so many critics.

MOBILIO: Given the general state of the literary climate—I don't know about in Russia, but certainly in the United States, and perhaps elsewhere—in which immediacy and clarity are the chief requirements for mass consumption, perhaps writing poetry is a utopian gesture in and of itself.

KUZNETSOVA: I wrote a poem last year with a fairly dystopian note. It makes reference to Plato working for the state and throwing the poets out of Athens, out of the polis. I'm not sure if Plato was depriving the poets of the benefits of citizenship, or if maybe he was in fact freeing them from the shackles of the state. In the poem, everything is gone except for one letter, and that letter, the remaining letter, is literature. And people no longer remember that poets were driven out beyond the gates of the city and that people stood on the city wall and hurled rocks and clumps of earth at them. But poets, the poem says, please, don't get upset. Because without any awards, without any attention or support, you can stroll freely outside the city walls, free to think of nothing but music.

MOBILIO: Perhaps in artistic expression there is a kind of achievable ideal—or at least as close as we can come. Eshkol, I was reading about your newest novel, which has yet to be translated into English, and apparently it's about a group of friends who exchange notes upon which they've written wishes. This put me in mind of what's done at the Wailing Wall, where prayers are inserted in the blocks of stone. And that seems in some way emblematic of the literary process, or at least a utopian-minded literary process: these short poems that express aspiration or hope passed among like-minded people.

NEVO: The starting point of that book is the World Cup of 1998. A bunch of friends are watching the finals, and one of them has an idea: Everyone will write down his three wishes for the forthcoming four years. It can be a wish about romantic life, professional life, maybe even a national wish. And they will take these notes and keep them hidden. After four years, at the next World Cup, they will open them and see what happens. This is the starting point, and then the book follows the wishes, and these four friends, and examines whether a wish you make, or a statement you make of what you want or of where you are heading—will it really end up being what you want? And the path you are going to walk? I think in Israel now there's a very popular—I don't know if it's still like that here, but there's a lot of…coaching? Coaches?

MOBILIO: A life coach, someone who helps you perfect yourself?

NEVO: Yes, yes. So if you sit in a café in Israel, you hear a lot of conversations between people and their coaches. They're all about goals and sub-goals and sub-sub-goals. The book is also about this idea. Is life really like that? Can you state your goals and your sub-goals, and then go ahead and fulfill them? The book looks at the stream of life and examines what it does to your wishes as time passes, as you grow up, as your country changes. After I wrote *Homesick*, which looks at the past and the longing for the past, I wanted to look ahead, towards the future—as a human being and as a writer. Writing about these wishes was also my wish. I wanted to write a book about what it is to think of a future, to go towards a future.

MOBILIO: One definition of utopia might be "rules for a provisional future." When we look at any number of literary utopias—Plato's Atlantis or Sir Thomas More's Utopia—these are places that are very rule-bound. Utopian novels, in fact, are mostly constituted of very specific, anal-retentive rules. And a good deal of writing seeks rules. We write in genres, we adopt poetic forms, we adopt particular narrative forms—first person, third person, diary. Jonathan, you play around a lot with genre. I wonder if you see a connection there?

LETHEM: Yeah, I really like the direction you're gesturing—and I think the key word is provisional. When you speak of rules, you're speaking of a world of games—things that are both artificial and temporary but can still be embraced. I think one way to embrace the notion of utopian longing is to try to take away the idea of utopia as something monolithic and indefinite and without boundaries, and instead look at it as a kind of zone of operation—a game that can be played successfully for a little while and may inevitably dissolve. The American anarchist philosopher Hakim Bey has this phrase: "temporary autonomous zones." What he has in mind are places like the Burning Man Festival, which arises according to a yearly schedule for a few days out in the desert. People gather and—with a concentrated, extremely deliberate, extremely artificial energy—create a temporary autonomous zone of utopia, where everything must be negotiated. It's very much like a game or a literary genre, where the apparatus is conscious and the construction of it is part of the pleasure. It's not meant to be naturalized, or finished, with the rule-making done, set to go on forever and be perfect. Instead, the making of it becomes the utopia. It is accepted that it will melt away, and the hope is that these moments of utopia can be asserted again and again.

Of course, that is what artistic practice is like, and that's what a poetry reading is like. That group of people, the same faces showing up, caring about the poems again and again, is, in a sense, one of those temporary autonomous zones. This panel itself could be taken as one. Here's a conversation across cultures happening in an extremely artificial and structured way—but no less beautiful for its artificiality or the fact that an hour later we'll all go off to our separate lives. It will still have been a kind of utopia.

MOBILIO: Just to play devil's advocate for a bit, Jonathan, while I agree with everything you've said about utopia as a set of temporary rules, I wonder if the reason I agree with you is that I, too, am a child of a country in which the rules often *can* be temporary—because they are subject to democratic process. And I wonder if, for instance, Andrzej or Inga might see the notion of rules, utopian or dystopian rules, as malleable as you or I might, or as the object of aesthetic play. Andrzej, what do you think?

STASIUK: I'm a bad example because I don't play games. I'm not really interested in rules. What I'm more interested in is the chaos of life that we try to recreate in literature. Again I have to speak about boredom. I've always been bored during games. I was never able to play cards or anything else. What I like is the lack of rules. I never liked literature that consisted of many rules. What I like is what I would call the real flesh of life. Maybe this is a kind of utopia. Maybe we do not live beyond games, but this is what I'd like to imagine—that we live without rules. Perhaps real life is a utopia; maybe it has the kind of rules that we try not to examine. It's a matter of temperament. Either it's the utopia of a game or it's the one of real life.

KUZNETSOVA: I understand well what Andrzej is saying. I don't know whether it's because we lived for a long time in very similar conditions, or whether it's for some other reason, but I also can't stand rules or games—or any kind of collective effort.

STASIUK: Let's not talk about collectives.

KUZNETSOVA: And what's going on here right now, this conversation, I don't perceive as a game or as something artificial. I perceive it as the opportunity to hear what's going on in the minds and hearts of those who are speaking. What we're talking about is what is important to us. We're talking about existence in the broad sense, and we are allowing each other to enter into each other's personal utopias. This is a global exercise, without barriers, without walls. It's like a field of thought, a cloud we can all move around in—and it's not important whether the conversation is intellectual or not. It's important that there's this thought-field that we are all in.

MOBILIO: I'm reminded of Lionel Trilling, who described New Yorkers as eight million people with their own personal Waldens—referring to Thoreau's rural utopian dwelling. Before opening things up to the audience, I want to return to Eshkol, and this idea of a nation springing from a novel—because I think that, as writers, we often are inclined to undervalue the power of literary expression. But then one thinks of Herzl's novel—or of Orwell's *Animal Farm*, which was absolutely formative; you could probably trace a line from Orwell to the fall of the Berlin Wall.

NEVO: As a writer, I don't have the aspiration of writing a novel that will formulate a country—but every writer, even if he denies it, has an aspiration to make an effect on the world. Coming back to *Homesick*: One of the things that happened with that novel is it became part of the education system in Israel. Which is embarrassing in a way, because now people have to take exams on this book. But, on the other hand, Israeli Jewish students in Israeli Jewish high schools are exposed to this Palestinian narrative of longing, which is almost a utopia itself in Israel—because that's not a subject talked about or learned in history lessons. So there's a student, and he goes to his history lesson, and hears one version—then maybe he goes to his literature lesson, and learns my book, and hears the perspective of the other. And he's probably confused, which is great. As a writer, I aspire to confuse, to raise questions—and it doesn't have to be in the political or social arena; it can be on an emotional level.

This book you talked about, my next book, *World Cup Wishes*, is about friendship—friendship as a value in a very capitalistic world. When somebody comes up to me or writes me a letter about the book and says, "I read your book, and then I called all my friends, and we met together, and it reminded me of friendship and how valuable it is," that's not founding a country, but it *is* doing something with your words. And if we were not aspiring to do something, I guess we wouldn't write. Because it's not only about our own amusement or our own zone. We enjoy the zone Jonathan was talking about—I definitely feel that zone when I am writing. But it's not only about this; you want to make an effect. I guess, in our times, you have to be more moderate in your aspirations, more realistic. But if you can touch someone, if you can make him stop for a moment and think about love, about friendship, about the place he is living in, about his relationships, about his family, then you have made something. It was worthwhile, not only for you, but also for your reader.

AUDIENCE: I have a question for Inga. Do you believe that poetry is more suitable for the description of utopias, and that prose is more connected to dystopias?

KUZNETSOVA: It doesn't make a difference. Any successful text, be it poetry or prose, is a utopia in and of itself, and such a text is simply far better organized than any social structure. At least, that's my anarchistic opinion on the matter.

AUDIENCE: I wonder if it's possible to write a utopia now, in the traditional sense of utopia—a future with a kind of naïve and innocent perfection. Even in young adult fiction now, visions of the future are almost exclusively dystopian. Is it possible in our age of irony to have that kind of naïve and purely positive view of the future?

NEVO: It's terribly difficult. I'm faced with a dilemma, because I have this belief that it's not good to talk about the book you're working on—but I have no choice now. I'm not writing a utopia, I'm not writing *Altneuland* again, but in a section of the book I am writing I try to describe a little place, not in Israel, which runs by certain rules, maybe utopian rules. It was very, very difficult to write. There was this cynical demon inside of me, laughing at me while I was writing all the time: "You can't be serious." But still I tried to do it. And I'm still in the middle of the process, so I don't know if I have done it or not. But it's definitely difficult and very, very complex to undertake as a writer nowadays.

STASIUK: I think that modern pop culture tries to make different utopias true. They offer us opportunities to create ourselves anew as a single human being. We could choose our own personality, we could choose how we look, and we could choose even our body structure, because you could still take different body organs. We could choose the model or the structure of our life, we could choose the place we want to live, the country we are going to live in. These are the offers and the proposals of pop culture, which to my mind are utopian.

KUZNETSOVA: One thing we cannot choose is the absence of death, unfortunately.

STASIUK: I think very soon we will be immortal.

KUZNETSOVA: I hope!

STASIUK: It's the next utopia that we are going to deal with, being immortal. When you think about what is being developed in biotechnology—I think this will happen in America, which is a huge and rich country.

MOBILIO: The magazine that I edit, *Bookforum*, is doing a special section inviting a number of writers to meditate on the notion of utopia, along with various scholars and scientists. One of the people we contacted is an architect designing a cryogenic palace, where bodies will be kept frozen for eternity—which is something, as Jonathan knows, that Philip K. Dick already imagined. But the architectural drawings are on the table. So you're right, America may very well pioneer the utopia of immortality.

KUZNETSOVA: Well, until the cryogenic palace exists, where bodies will be preserved frozen until they can be reanimated, in our present conditions, the only way, still, to achieve immortality is to write a really good work of literature.

FICTION

BEFORE THE NEXT WORLD CUP

Eshkol Nevo

Translated by Sondra Silverston

It was Amichai's idea, those wishes.

After Emanuel Petit scored the third goal and it was already clear that France would take the Cup, and there was a faint sense of disappointment in the air because we were all rooting for Brazil, after we'd finished off the tear-flavored burekas Ilana had baked and the last nut had been cracked and only one piece of the watermelon and feta cheese was left, the piece no one felt comfortable taking—after all that, Ofir said, you know, something just hit me. This is the fifth World Cup we're watching together. And Churchill said, how do you figure five? Four, tops.

And we started going over them.

Mexico '86 we saw in Ofir's father's house in Tivon. And when poor, naïve Denmark lost five-one to Spain, Ofir cried his heart out and his father said that's what happens when a boy is raised by his mother. The '90 World Cup we each saw in a different city in the territories, but there was one Saturday when we all went home and met at Amichai's place to watch the semifinal. No one remembered who played because his little sister was walking around the house in red baby-dolls and we were soldiers and couldn't keep our eyes on the screen. In '94, we were students. Tel Avivians. Churchill was the first to move there, and we all trailed after him to the big city because we wanted to stay together and because Churchill said that it was the only place where we could be what we wanted to be.

But we actually saw the '94 games in Rambam hospital in Haifa, Ofir remembered. Ri-i-ght, I said.

In the middle of supper at my parents' place, I had the worst wheezing asthma attack of my life. There were moments in the panicky ride to the hospital when I was seriously considering dying. After they stabilized me with injections and pills and an oxygen mask, the doctors said I had to stay in the hospital for the next few days. For observation.

The final was the next day. Italy against Brazil. Without telling me, Churchill got the guys together and put them all into his wrinkled Beetle, and on the way, they stopped at the Pancake House in Kfar Vitkin to buy me peach-flavored iced tea because that's my particular passion, and a couple of bottles of vodka, because in those days we pretended to be into vodka, and ten minutes before the match started, they burst loudly into my hospital room (they bribed the guard with a bottle of Keglevich when he tried to stop them because visiting hours were over). I almost had another attack when I saw them. But then I calmed down and breathed deeply, from the diaphragm, and together we watched the tiny TV hanging above my bed and saw Brazil take the cup after 120 minutes. Plus penalty kicks.

And...so we came to '98, Churchill summed up. Four World Cups altogether.

It's a lucky thing we didn't bet, Ofir said.

It's a lucky thing there's a World Cup, I said. That way, time doesn't turn into one big, solid block, and we can stop every four years and see what's changed.

Awesome, Churchill said. He was always the first one to understand when I came up with a remark like that. Sometimes the only one.

You know what's lucky? It's lucky that we have each other, Ofir said. You have n-o-o i-ide-ea how lucky we are, we completed the familiar remark.

Bro, I don't understand how you manage with all those ad men, you're such a pussy, Churchill said, and Ofir laughed, OK, that's what happens when you grow up with your mother, and Amichai said, I have an idea.

Wait, let's just watch them hoist the cup, Churchill said, hoping that by the time they were finished hoisting the cup, he'd forget his idea.

But Amichai didn't forget.

Did he know that the idea he was about to suggest would turn out to be a true prophecy that would disappoint us time after time over the next four years, and amazingly enough, would preserve its prophetic power?

What I was thinking, he said, is that we should each write down on a piece of paper where we dream of being in another four years. Personally, professionally. In every sense. And at the next World Cup, we'll open the papers and see what happened in the meantime.

OK, I said. Bring paper.

But let's be organized, Churchill said. Everyone writes three things. Three short sentences. Otherwise, there'll be no end to it.

Amichai passed out thick psychology books so we'd have something to rest the paper on. And pens.

I had no problem with the first wish. It had formed itself in my mind the minute Amichai tossed out the idea.

At the next World Cup, I still want to be with Ya'ara, I wrote.

Then I got stuck. I tried to think of other things I wanted to wish for myself, I tried to expand the scope of my desires, but my thoughts kept going back to her, to her silky, caramel-colored hair, her soft slender shoulders, those green eyes of hers encircled by glasses, the moment she takes them off and I know we can.

We'd met two months earlier in the cafeteria in the Naftali building on campus. At the beginning of the break, she came in with two guys, carrying a large tray with a small bottle of grapefruit juice on it. She walked with her back straight, a brisk walk that made her caramel-colored ponytail bounce, as if she were in a hurry to go somewhere else, and they lurched heavily along behind her to the table. She had trouble opening the bottle of juice, but didn't ask for help. They were talking about a play they'd seen the night before. That is, she was talking, very quickly, and they were looking at her. She said that they could've done a lot more with that play if the director had only had a little inspiration. For instance the scenery, she said and sipped her juice, why do the stage sets in this country always look the same? Can't they think of something a little more original than a table, coat hooks, and an armchair from the flea market? She kept talking—about the music and how the director could have got more from the actors if he'd done his job out of a real love for the profession. She stretched out the 'o' in "love," pronouncing the word with all her heart, and as she said it, placed her open hand on her shirt. That is so-o-o true, the guy sitting across from her said without taking his eyes off her shirt. You're absolutely right, Ya'ara, the other guy said. Then both guys got up and went to their class, leaving her sitting alone at the table, and suddenly, for a fraction of a second, she looked small and lost. She took some papers out of her bag, pushed her glasses more firmly onto her nose with her pinky, crossed her legs, and became engrossed in reading. Every time she turned a page, she touched a finger lightly to her tongue, and I watched her, thinking how incredible it was that such a gesture, a librarian's gesture, could be sexy on the right girl. And I also thought that it would be interesting to know what that serious face looked like when she burst out laughing. And if she had dimples. And I thought that I'd never know, because I'd never have the guts to come on to her.

Hey, she said, looking up from the pages, you have any idea what the English word "revelation" means?

Every impairment has its moment of glory. Years of a spartan Anglo-Saxon education, a wildly exaggerated amount of tea with milk, chronic emotional constipation and a basic sense of alienation instilled in me because my parents never stopped feeling like outsiders here, in the Levant, and kept speaking Anglicized Hebrew to each other for thirty years after arriving in Haifa from Brighton—

All those, for one moment, worked to my benefit.

I explained to her authoritatively in Hebrew that revelation meant exposure or disclosure, and when I saw that she was satisfied with my answer and was about to go back to her reading, I quickly added that it could also mean "epiphany." Depending on the context.

She read me the whole sentence. Then another sentence she had trouble with. So I gave her my phone number, in case she needed more help, and, amazingly enough, she called that same night and we talked about other things too, and the conversation flowed like wine, and then we went out, and kissed, and made love, and she put her head on my stomach when we were lying on the grass near the Music Academy and tapped on my thigh to a piano melody that was coming from one of the rehearsal rooms, and bought me a turquoise shirt because "enough with all that black," and I kept looking for the trap that whole time, how could it be that a girl who disproves Churchill's three-quarters theory—"There are no girls who are pretty and smart and horny and also available. One of these elements is always missing"—how could it be that a girl like that would pick me, of all people? True, a few months before she met me, she split with a guitarist who had made her miserable with five years of cheating on her, then begging her to take him back, but there were enough guys wandering around campus who were taller than me and would have been happy to be a corrective experience for her. And anyway, that whole story with the cheating guitarist didn't make sense. Who would want to cheat on someone like her? Who would ever want anything but more and more of her?

Amichai pushed me to finish. Everyone but me had already given back the pens.

I looked at the first sentence I'd written and added impulsively:

2. At the next World Cup, I want to be married to Ya'ara.

3. At the next World Cup, I want to have a child with Ya'ara. Ideally a girl.

Now you give me the slips of paper, Amichai said. And I keep them closed in a box till the next World Cup.

Why you? Ofir objected.

Because I'm the most stable guy here.

What does that mean? Ofir said, getting angry.

He's right, Churchill said, trying to soften it. He has a wife, an apartment, twins. We'll probably go through ten apartments till the next World Cup, and slips of paper like these are just the kind of thing that gets lost in packing.

OK, Ofir said. But let's read them out loud first.

Are you kidding?! Amichai shouted. That kills the whole surprise.

Fuck the surprise, Ofir said angrily. I want to know what you all wrote. Otherwise, I won't give you mine.

Delayed gratification isn't exactly your thing, is it? Amichai said sarcastically, then added casually, well, this is what happens when a kid is raised by his mother.

You know the story about the man who delayed gratification? Ofir shot back. There's a guy who delays gratification. Delays, delays, delays—then he dies.

I have an idea, Churchill interrupted before Ofir and Amichai got carried away into one of their verbal clashes, sudden, meaningless clashes that brought out a nastiness it was hard to believe they were capable of. How about if everyone reads only one of the three things he wrote, Churchill said. That way we can keep the element of surprise and we'll still have the teasing. That is what you advertising guys call it, right?

Teaser, Ofir corrected, and a shadow crossed his eyes, the way it did every time someone mentioned his work.

Okay, I'll go first, Amichai said, unfolding his slip of paper.

At the next World Cup, I'll have an alternative therapy clinic.

A-a-men, Churchill prayed, putting into words what all of us felt. If it came true, we hoped, perhaps Amichai would stop talking about it so much.

Ofir unfolded his slip of paper.

At the next World Cup, I'll kiss the advertising world goodbye and publish a book of short stories.

Short stories? I said, surprised. Didn't you say you were going to make a movie about us?

Yes, Ofir, said, but the whole movie was based on the idea that one of us... dies in the army. And you promised that if no one did, then...

If it's still an option, I'm ready to die any time, I offered (and as I did, a too-pleasant shiver ran through me, as it always did when I thought about the possibility.)

Forget it, Ofir said. It's not necessary. Lately, I'm more into the short story thing. My head is full of ideas, but when I get home from the office at eleven at night, I don't even have the energy to turn on the computer.

So yallah, I urged him, move your ass. You have time till the next World Cup. In any case, you already have an English translator.

Thanks man, he said and patted me on the shoulder, his eyes glistening. You have no idea how lucky...

Churchill quickly unfolded his slip of paper before Ofir could start weeping.

By the next World Cup, he said in a very serious tone, I plan to have slept with at least 208 girls.

Exactly 208? Amichai said with a laugh. Why not 222? Or a round 300?

Do the numbers, Churchill explained. Four years, fifty-two weeks a year. One girl a week—a total of 208. Just kidding. You really think I'd waste a wish on something that's going to happen anyway?

So what, then, you were just playing us? Amichai asked, his voice dropping. For a person doomed to one Ilana the Weeper, the thought of a wish that included 208 different women must have lit up his imagination.

Obviously, Churchill said with a laugh and read from his list:

By the next World Cup, I want to have an important case. In an important area. I want to be involved in something that will lead to social change.

Ofir and Amichai nodded in admiration and I thought to myself that it was a little embarrassing to read one of my wishes out loud after what Churchill had just read.

Okay, your turn now, Amichai said to me. I looked at the slip of paper and took comfort in the fact that at least I didn't have to read all three.

At the next World Cup, I want to be with Ya'ara, I read in a fading voice.

And as expected, everyone attacked me.

Yallah, yallah, that Ya'ara doesn't even exist, Ofir said.

Till we see her, that wish isn't valid, Churchill added a legal opinion.

I think she's probably ugly, I think he's keeping her under wraps because she's ugly, Ofir said and looked at me to see if I was annoyed.

Cross-eyed blind, Amichai said.

With an ass the size of a helicopter pad.

Tits down to her knees.

Football player shoulders.

She's probably a man who had a sex change operation. Before that, they called her Ya'ar.

Oka-a-a-y, I said, I give up. You're all invited to my place on Tuesday to meet her.

But on that Monday, I put off the meeting for a week with the excuse that I was sick, and I cancelled the postponed meeting too, saying that we had to be at her parents' house in Rehovot for dinner, and finally, the one who put an end to all those postponements was Ya'ara herself, who told me, one-third as a joke and two-thirds seriously, I'm starting to think you're ashamed of me. Don't be silly, I said. Then why don't you introduce me to your friends, she asked. No reason, I replied, it just hasn't worked out. And she said, I'm dying to meet them. You talk about them so much. And I said, I never noticed. You mention them in practically every sentence, she said. And your living room is full of pictures of them, out-of-focus pictures, but still. And every five minutes, one of them calls you, and then you get into long, deep conversations with them. Not the kind of practical conversations men have, but real conversations. It just seems to me that you all have a very strong connection, right?

I don't know, I said. Sometimes I think we do. That it's for our whole lives. Like a year ago, we went back to our school for the Memorial Day ceremony and I noticed that all the other groups of friends from our grade had broken up, and we were the only ones standing there together, close, during the siren. And the truth is that I have no idea why. Whether it's inertia or whether even now, after eight years in Tel Aviv, we still only feel like we belong when we're together. But there are other times when I don't understand what we're doing together, like there's no reason for it. But maybe that's how it is, and that endless dance of getting close and growing apart is just the basic movement among friends. What do you think?

A fa-a-a-scinating analysis, Ya'ara said, but don't change the subject. Next Tuesday we're cooking them dinner, she said firmly, and took off her glasses. And I said okay because it's hard to say no to green eyes and because I couldn't find a good reason to object, except for the vague feeling I had that it would end in tears, a feeling I attributed to my chronic pessimism.

But the dinner was actually a great success. They devoured the stuffed vegetables we made, and Ya'ara easily found a common language with each of the guys. She laughed with Ofir about the whole world of advertising (it turns out that she once worked as an assistant producer on the set of a laundry detergent ad that was being shot). She argued with Churchill about the leniency the prosecutor's office showed towards public figures. She told Amichai about the acupuncture treatment that cured her—to the amazement of her conventional doctors—of mononucleosis. And she kept touching me the whole time, rubbed the back of my neck, put her hand on mine, her head on my shoulder, and twice she even kissed me lightly on the neck, as if she suddenly sensed what I had been trying to hide from her through all the months we'd been together: that I was afraid of losing her. That I'd never had anything like us before.

So? I asked when they'd gone. We could still hear their footsteps on the landing.

They're terrific, your friends, Ya'ara said and hugged me.

Explain, I said, and went to wash the dishes. Two or three stuffed vegetable corpses were still stuck to the plates.

That Ofir is so sensitive, I heard her voice behind me. How many years has he been in advertising? Six? It's not easy to stay who you are in that cynical world. And Amichai, that guy has so much patience. I think he really could be a great alternative therapist. And all of them, she said and hugged me from behind, seem to love you very much. So we all have at least one thing in common.

And Churchill? I asked, and I could feel her loosen her grip, then drop her hands.

Seems like a smart guy, she said in a hesitant voice.

But…? I turned around to face her. My hands were still wet with dish-washing soap.

No buts, she said, moving away a little.

It had the sound of a but, I insisted.

Forget it, it's not fair to judge after one time.

I knew she was right. And that it was much easier to label a person than to stay open to the possibility that there's more than one side to him. But I couldn't help it.

Come on, say it, I asked. I've known him for so many years that I can't tell anymore what kind of first impression he makes.

The truth is that there's something conceited about him. As if he's looking down at the three of you. From the VIP box. I don't like that. And I don't like the way he talks about women either. Did you notice that whenever he talked about male politicians, he called them "Minister" or "Mayor," and when he talked about women politicians, it was "the airhead" and "the bottle blond?"

Could be, I said coldly. And even though I'd asked for it, I felt the anger rise up in me at how insufferably easy it was for her to badmouth my friend. You should know that he's a special person, I shot the words at her. When he graduated from law school, he had offers from private firms that would have paid him a lot of money, but he went to the prosecutor's office because he thought it was more important, and a few weeks ago, at the World Cup final, we each wrote down on a slip of paper where we dream of being at the next World Cup, in four years. We all wrote totally egotistical things, and he was the only one who wanted to do something significant that would affect Israeli society, so… maybe you should wait a little before you decide what he's like.

What did you write? Ya'ara asked. Her eyes were seductive above her glasses. That was the first time since we'd started dating that I let myself be a little angry at her, and strangely enough, she seemed to like it.

It's a secret, I said, trying to keep a certain meanness in my tone. If you want to know, you'll have to stay with me till the next World Cup. That's when we read the slips of paper.

No problem, Ya'ara said, pressing up against me and putting her hands into the back pockets of my jeans, you can't scare a romantic girl with love.

Two weeks later, she was with him.

There are a few contradictory versions of how that happened.

Churchill claims that she bumped into him on the street, during his lunch break, and told him she thought they'd had a communications failure during dinner, and if he was up for it, she'd like to buy him a cup of coffee so they could start over. He agreed, because he felt it was important to her. So they sat in a café and talked and didn't notice the time passing. And in the end, when they stood up to go, she said there were a lot of things they'd talked about that were left open and perhaps they should meet again the next day to close them.

Ya'ara claims that he was the one who called her, three days after the dinner, and said that ever since he met her, he hadn't been able to stop thinking about her and couldn't fall asleep at night. She told him she didn't know what to say, and he said he wanted to see her. She said, what are you talking about, they couldn't do something like that behind my back. But he pleaded with her and said that a lot of criminals, rapists and murderers, were walking out of court free men because he hadn't been able to function since he met her. She laughed and agreed to see him, just for a few minutes, just for coffee, just because of the rapists. After coffee, when they got up to go, he said that there were a lot of things they'd talked about that were still left open, and perhaps they should meet again the next day to close them.

I imagine that she was probably telling the truth.

I'd like to believe that he was telling the truth.

LIVES

Arthur Rimbaud

Translated by John Ashbery

1

O the enormous avenues of the holy land, the terraces of the temple! What have they done with the brahmin who was explaining the Proverbs to me? From that time, from back then, I still see even the old women! I remember the hours of silver and sun toward the rivers, the hand of the countryside on my shoulder, and our caresses as we stood in the pepper-scented plain. —A flight of scarlet pigeons roars around my thought— Exiled here I had a stage on which to act out the dramatic masterpieces of all the literatures. I would show you undreamed-of riches. I observe the history of the treasures you found. I see what comes afterward! My wisdom is as spurned as chaos. What is my nothingness, compared to the amazement that awaits you?

2

I am an inventor altogether more deserving than all those who have preceded me; a musician, in fact, who has discovered something like the key of love. At present, squire of a sour country with a sober sky, I try to be touched by the memory of a childhood spent begging, of apprenticeship or my arrival in wooden shoes, of polemics, of five or six widowings, and several wedding parties where my obstinate head prevented me from rising to the fever pitch of my pals. I don't miss my old role in divine merrymaking: the sober air of this sour countryside is ample nourishment for my hideous skepticism. But as this skepticism can now never be transformed into action, and since I'm now dedicated to a new turmoil, —I'm waiting to become a most wicked madman.

3

In an attic where I was shut up at the age of twelve I got to know the world, I illustrated the human comedy. In a cellar I learned history. At some night-time carnival in a Northern city, I met all the wives of the master painters. In an old arcade in Paris I was taught the classic sciences. In a magnificent abode surrounded by the entire Orient I accomplished my immense opus and spent my illustrious retirement. I churned my blood. My homework has been handed back to me. One mustn't even think of that now. I'm really beyond the grave, and no more assignments, please.

LOVERS: A FORUM

Continued from page 19

RECOGNITIONS | MARILYNNE ROBINSON

When I was in college, it was my good fortune to be a student of John Hawkes. Momentously for me, he once put a blessing on a paragraph of mine. He called it Proustian. He did this to shelter it from the criticisms of my fellow students, who were aflame then with a stern undergraduate passion for truth-telling, for tearing away veils and dispelling illusions. I was as impressed by this project as anyone, and I made certain poor attempts at it, which the formidable Mr. Hawkes discouraged by invoking this great name to approve one straying memory of my primordial Idaho.

I had read no Proust at the time. I was much struck by the freedom from constraint and expectation I suddenly enjoyed. Thereafter, I could complicate my sentences and elaborate my metaphors and explore my memory without prosecutorial intent, and still be respected by my peers. I learned a true thing then, that no one is ever in advance of Proust. The most radical aesthetic will always accept him as an honored contemporary and collaborator. So I associated Proust with the blessing and freeing of language and memory and of the testimony of the individual spirit, even before I discovered by reading him that he should indeed be associated with just these things.

AERIAL MANEUVERS | UMBERTO ECO

I want to explain how, when I was a young man of twenty-five, reading Calvino's *The Baron in the Trees* had such a powerful impact on my notions of political engagement and the social role of intellectuals.

It goes without saying that the book delighted me as a stupendous work of

The pieces that appear on pages 204-212 all originally appeared, some in longer form, in *PEN America* issues 1-9, published between 2001 and 2008. For more, visit **www.pen.org/journal**.

literature, making me dream of those enchanted woods of Ombrosa sloping triumphantly down toward the sea. I reread the novel and felt the same impression
of felicity, enchanted once more by the spell of a transparent language through
which I felt myself, in a quasi-physical way, climbing from branch to branch
with Cosimo, and becoming successively a golden oriole, a squirrel, a wild cat, a
sparrow, even a cherry and an olive leaf. The language of *The Baron* is crystalline,
and in *Six Memos for the Next Millennium* Calvino said that the crystal, with its
precise faceting and its ability to refract light, was the model of perfection that
he always cherished as an emblem.

But in 1957 my main reaction was philosophical rather than aesthetic,
which shouldn't amaze anyone. I was not reading a fairy tale, as many considered it, but a great conte philosophique.

The young intellectuals of the '40s and '50s, whether Communist or
Catholic, were obsessed with the moral duty to be, as they used to say, "organic"
to their own ideological group. One felt blackmailed by the general call to
be militant and rally one's intellectual power against the ideological enemies.
Only two voices offered another conception. The first was Elio Vittorini, who
would later collaborate with Calvino on *Il Menabò*, a journal which profoundly
influenced the course of Italian literature in the '60s. In 1947 Vittorini said that
intellectuals must not play the flute for the revolution: Rather than act as press
agents for their political group, they must become its critical consciousness.
Vittorini belonged at that time to the Communist Party and published a rather
independent and short-lived journal, *Il Politecnico*. Obviously, he was considered
a traitor to the working class. *Il Politecnico* died, and Vittorini's appeal remained,
for a long time, unheard.

I remember that years later, during one of those overheated student meetings of 1968, when I was asked to define the role of the intellectual, I proposed
Calvino's novel as the only reliable textbook. Quoting Cosimo as a model, I
said that the first duty of engaged intellectuals was to live in the trees, to keep
a distance from their companions in order to criticize them. Their second duty
was not to provide slogans against their adversaries. I also said that intellectuals
must be ready to face a firing squad. At that time this was not a popular view,
but many of the students who booed then went on to work for Berlusconi.

Why was the lesson suggested by this novel so convincing to me? Aerial
like his Baron, Calvino's prose has no weight; it is "plus vague et plus soluble
dans l'air, sans rien en lui qui pèse ou qui pose," as Verlaine would have said. Or,
to conclude with Calvino's words: "Whenever humanity seems condemned to
heaviness, I think I should fly like Perseus into a different space. I don't mean

escaping into dreams or into the irrational. I mean that I have to change my approach, look at the world from a different perspective, with a different logic and with fresh methods of cognition and verification. The image of lightness that I seek should not fade away like dreams dissolved by the realities of present and future…"

TO CHANGE THE WORLD | RUSSELL BANKS

Though I never met James Baldwin in person, and never even saw him at a public event, he is nonetheless to me like a father, or a beloved uncle, or mentor. That is to say, he is in my mind nearly every day, for the very simple reason that he was instrumental in creating my mind. And to the degree that my life and work have been shaped by my mind, especially in the way it is positioned with regard to race in America, James Baldwin shaped that life and work. Our actual lives never touched, except through his words, which is the most intimate touch of all. And his words expressed in those early essays which later became *Nobody Knows My Name* and *The Fire Next Time* entered my life at a time when I was a very young man, impressionable, confused, ignorant, and emotionally turbulent. Still a boy, actually, a well-intended white New Englander who had romanticized his sweetly naïve but pragmatically useless youthful idealism so that he could take pride in it, so that he could think better of himself, seated somewhat uncomfortably in a guilt-drenched 1950s white-boy garden of privilege.

However, although I had almost no idea of how to go about becoming either, I wanted to become a writer and a good person. I was a pipe fitter in New Hampshire then with no college and little travel—an unpromising situation. But thanks to my fuzzy, self-serving idealism, and my twin desires to become a writer and a good person, I was reading in those days—the late 1950s, early 1960s—periodicals like *Partisan Review*, where I read for the first time the mind-altering essay "Nobody Knows My Name: A Letter from the South." And then the brilliant dissection "Faulkner and Desegregation," troubling to me, for Faulkner had already been at work creating my mind for several years. I was also reading *The Progressive* (possibly the only person in Concord, New Hampshire, at that time, certainly the only pipe fitter), where I came upon "My Dungeon Shook: Letter to My Nephew on the One Hundredth Anniversary of the Emancipation." And then one unforgettable night, I read in *The New Yorker*, transfixed and transformed, the long essay that we remember now as "The Fire Next Time," called there, "Letter from a Region in My Mind."

Baldwin's words, his language, trickled into my ear, and became an inner voice that woke me suddenly from a long, mind-numbing, conscience-killing slumber. I can imagine, many generations earlier, a young New England boy reading Emerson for the first time, and feeling, thinking, as I did on first reading James Baldwin: Here was the undeniable, inescapable truth of the matter, and Good God, it was right in front of my eyes all along, and I never saw it. You felt as if you had been blind and were suddenly given sight, or foolish and had suddenly been given sense. It's so easy when you are a white man in America to remain blind to what lies in front of you, and a fool. How ashamed, yet wonderfully liberated I was, when I read this sentence, for example, among many others: "White people in this country will have quite enough to do in learning how to accept and love themselves and each other, and when they have achieved this—which will not be tomorrow, and may very well be never—the Negro problem will no longer exist, for it will no longer be needed."

I could feel my heart and head clear together. My thoughts and pulse racing from premise to conclusion at the speed of light, it seemed, as I sat in my rented room and read not quite by candlelight, but in the dim glow of a bedside lamp, Baldwin's elucidation of the so-called Negro student movement, the earliest manifestation of what soon became the civil rights movement—an elucidation that gave me leave, a few years later, to cleave in my own feeble way to the work too. "The goal of the student movement," he wrote, "is nothing less than the liberation of the entire country from its most crippling attitudes and habits. The reason that it is of the utmost importance for white people, here, to see the Negroes as people like themselves is that white people will not otherwise be able to see themselves as they are."

I truly wished to see myself as I was, and to the degree that I have been successful in this, Baldwin taught me how. His aphoristic style, his mixture of high diction and low, the rhetoric of the pulpit and of the street, his willingness to take the universe personally, his uneasy relationship with Christianity—these are qualities he shares with Emerson, one of my earlier fathers, and in fact I believe that Baldwin's essays can stand easily alongside Emerson's. Because there lies, at the center of Baldwin's thinking, the central fact of the American imagination, which is race, his essays in the end will go further toward the shaping of the American imagination than those of any other writer so far, and will do so for generations to come.

"You write in order to change the world," Baldwin said, "knowing perfectly well that you probably can't, but also knowing that literature is indispensable to the world. The world changes according to the way people see it, and if you alter even by a millimeter the way people look at reality, then you can change it." His heart was a target of opportunity, and he suffered terribly for it, but James Baldwin changed the world.

THE DAY I FINALLY MET BALDWIN | CHINUA ACHEBE

When I encountered James Baldwin's books, they blew my mind. I wanted very much to meet this man with the fearlessness of Old Testament prophets and the clarity, eloquence, and intelligence of ancient African griots. My chance to meet Baldwin finally came almost two decades later, in 1980. The occasion was an annual conference of the African Literature Association. The association had invited Baldwin and me to open their conference with a conversation. Everything was going swimmingly. The tone was joyful and also serious. With typical hyperbole, Baldwin called me his buddy, a brother he had not seen in four hundred years.

He said there were only twenty years to a new century. And he said he would be there, because he was stubborn. But, as we all know, he did not make it. He did not even make it to the University of Massachusetts at Amherst, which had invited him and me for the fall semester in 1987. Our conversation had been stopped for good. Or has it?

Literal-minded people have always had trouble with the language of prophets. As when Baldwin says to his nephew, "You come from a long line of great poets, some of the greatest poets since Homer. One of them said, 'The very time I thought I was lost, my dungeon shook and my chains fell off.'"

A bitter critic accused Baldwin of encouraging Black Nationalist automatons in the belief that they were descendants of kings and queens, and should therefore uncritically identify with Africa. Baldwin did not advocate uncritical identification with anything. At one point in his life, he compared his African heritage most adversely with the heritage of humble Swiss peasants. "Out of their hymns and dances came Beethoven and Bach. Go back a few centuries and they are in their full glory—but I am in Africa, watching the conquerors arrive." Those are not the words of uncritical advocacy. The difference between Baldwin and some of his critics is that he was not scared of anybody or anything. He was not even scared of Africa.

WORD-LINKED | COLUM McCANN

The best literature is connected. We are word-linked. What gives off the deepest sparks is that democracy of storytelling. The finest writers are those who, when we hear them for the very first time, sound as if they've been whispering in our ears our whole lives. Somehow, they've always been there; somehow, they always will be. Their words unravel and remake us. We enter a world we did not know, an imaginative elsewhere. We become alive in bodies not our own, and the luckiest of us emerge into an old world that we again do not recognize. Things fall apart, things come together.

A language was forced on the people around Chinua Achebe, just as a language was forced upon those around Yeats and Leopold Senghor and James Joyce and Aimé Césaire and James Baldwin and countless others down through the years. When they began to talk back; when they got up in the face of that language; when they caught the words in mid-flight and they returned them—they did so with a different accent. Literature had been such a one-sided, one-curtained conversation for so many years that when a book like *Things Fall Apart* appeared, we knew; in Ireland; in Korea; in New York—we knew that the so-called rest of the world could rip the cloth and open up the window. That's what Chinua Achebe did. He opened up the windows of his room, his own room, his own story. And he created in that space an everywhere. He made the local the universal and helped us all to change our voices. He himself said, wonderfully: "If you don't like someone's story, tell your own."

GRACENESS | MICHAEL CUNNINGHAM

There is a small body of writers—to my mind, the greatest writers—whose voices on paper are so distinct, so utterly their own, that we can identify them by one or two lines. For instance: "She was a woman of mean understanding, little information, and uncertain temper. When she was discontented, she fancied herself nervous. The business of her life was to get her daughters married; its solace was visiting and news." That would, of course, be Jane Austen. Then there's this: "There would be the dim coffin-smelling gloom sweet and oversweet with the twice-bloomed wisteria against the outer wall by the savage quiet September sun impacted distilled and hyperdistilled, into which came now and then the loud cloudy flutter of the sparrows." That is our own William Faulkner. And how about this: "Just when I most needed important conversation, a sniff of the man-wide world, that is, at least one brainy companion who could translate my friendly language into his tongue of undying carnal love, I was forced to lounge in our neighborhood park, surrounded by children." Hmm, who would that be?

Grace Paley was possessed of a voice so potent and magical, so off-hand and yet pitch-perfect, that I'm afraid I'd only embarrass myself by talking about it in much detail. Suffice it to say that her voice *came* from somewhere— politically outraged, female, multi-ethnic New York. And that mattered as much, and as little, as Austen's aristocratic England or Faulkner's crumbling south. Grace took the locutions of her time and place and spun them into, well, *Graceness*, which is the best term I have for a simple-sounding, but, in fact, quite complex vocabulary and syntax that enabled her to write unflinchingly and unapologetically about sex, love, birth, childrearing, housecleaning, marriage, divorce, aging, parents, and mortality, among other subjects. And to do so with the conviction, given all that people have gone through, that nothing is too trivial to merit a writer's serious attention—and nothing is so appalling that it isn't at least a little bit funny.

ARTIST OF THE PIXEL | PHILIP GOUREVITCH

Ryszard Kapuściński was a prose poet of great disorientations. He described being in a place in terms of being lost. He would wander into the mists of Siberia or stand in a sandstorm in the western Sahara or miss an inauguration in Uganda because he'd become afflicted with malaria. He was a kind of surrealist, a Chaplinesque figure with a fine-tuned sense of the absurd—and of pleasure.

It was as the Chaplin tramp of twentieth-century foreign correspondents that he gave us his greatest truths. He went into the world unprotected, and shared very closely in the conditions of the people that he was writing about. He went through a roadblock much as they went through a roadblock. It wasn't simply that he made himself insignificant; he knew that in such a place he *was* insignificant. Life was cheap, his own as much as anybody else's. He had no support system—there were no grounds for being grandiose. And this, I think, is a very difficult lesson for foreign correspondents, who don't want to sound frivolous, and who find themselves in places filled with darkness, where people are showing their passions and where history is being formed hourly, even by the minute, all around them. There is a tremendous excitement for somebody who is attuned to that, and who is aware of his own insignificance and not too troubled by it. That place is a place of pleasure for Kapuściński. It is a place where somebody who isn't rooted and who isn't home much has a chance to look around and see humanity and fate play out clearly around him.

LANGUAGE OF LABYRINTH | ROBERT STONE

A young aspiring writer, I discovered the work of Borges at about the same time that I began to read Beckett. Neither of these writers indicated directions

I believed that I would ever attempt to follow, yet I found them tremendously liberating and inspiring. Years later it fell to me to teach a fiction course that included an examination of Borges's work. What I learned from trying to teach that course was more of what I had already experienced in looking in those two different directions: the one leading to Beckett, and the other to Borges. The journey toward Beckett led to a turf-covered blasted heath, where language constantly seemed to fail, where life flickered on with language failing it—a place very much like the world. Borges's direction led to great vaults, a labyrinth, a labyrinth perhaps without a center, but filled with language, filled with narrative, an enormous quantity of invisible light, black light, an infinite passage of narrative over narrative upon narrative. Also a place very much like the world.

LAUGHTER IN THE DARK | PAUL AUSTER

I had the good fortune to meet Beckett a few times in Paris—several one-on-one conversations with him that lasted hours—and to have corresponded with him over the years. There's just one story I want to tell because it made such a deep impression on me and it taught me so much about what it means to be a writer. It took place during our first meeting in the early '70s, when I was about twenty-five years old. And at some point during the conversation, Beckett told me that he had just finished translating *Mercier et Camier*, which was his first French novel; it had been written about twenty-five years earlier.

I had read the book in French and liked it very much, and I said, "A wonderful book." I was just a kid, after all. I couldn't suppress my enthusiasm.

Beckett shook his head and said, "Oh no, no, not very good. In fact, I've cut out about twenty-five percent of the original. The English version's going to be a lot shorter than the French."

And I said (remember how young I was), "Why would you do such a thing? It's a wonderful book. You shouldn't have taken a word out."

He shook his head and he said, "No, no, not very good, not very good."

We went on to talk about other things, and then, out of the blue, ten or fifteen minutes later, apropos of nothing, he leaned forward across the table and he said to me, very earnestly, "You really liked it, huh? You really thought it was good?"

This was Samuel Beckett, remember. And not even he had any idea of what his work was worth. Good or bad, meaningful or not, no writer ever knows, not even the best ones. And I suppose especially not the best ones.

A SUFFERING CONSCIENCE | ARTHUR MILLER

A good writer helps to create other writers, and I can recall the first time, in the '30s, when I read John Steinbeck's early books, and his stories. To open those pages was like opening paintings. I remember clearly the challenge I felt to enter into nature, something I had never thought of before, coming from New York City. And I began to look around in Ann Arbor, Michigan, at trees, and animals, and I felt more alive because of his prose.

I thought of him as a friend, but our lives ran parallel, and with one or two exceptions they never really crossed. I had read him in college, and by the time we met in the early '50s, he was a world celebrity whose life was filled with famous friends, and the powers that come with fame. Such was the view from afar. But close up, it was his uncertainty I found surprising, and his shyness and sensitivity, especially when he was so physically large, and so deliberative in his views.

We lived in a time distorted by obligatory and defensive patriotism, in the '50s—an atmosphere which seems to be incubating again, incidentally. The contest then, however, was with the Russians, and it grew uglier by the week. John, after all, had begun as a radical writer, and the guilts inherent in that kind of alienation were compounded by the strident demands of convention in the '50s and later. It was perhaps inevitable, given the near-hysterical state worship of the hour, that he should have come to feel alien to both past and present ideologies. Filled with feeling, he tended to seek out the reassurance of goodness in the American world.

LAYING IT DOWN | WILLIE PERDOMO

I found Langston behind his typewriter the year after Ed Randolph, my first mentor, gave me poetry so I could stop fighting in a Quaker school. Freshman year Joyce and Piri Thomas were required reading in Mr. Byrne's lit class, but I took the liberty of putting Langston on my financial-aid voucher. That night, taking breaks from algebra, I heard the dogs in the street bark, couples argued, kids were being called in for dinner, and I went through those selected poems like I was stranded in a desert and a chilled bottle of Poland Spring water fell from the sky. I had a pop-up book in my hand, complete with the language to get around Lenox Avenue, to talk with the Madam, to play bop rim shots, to get inside the revolution, and to fall in love. Here I was, walking down the block with brand new ears, big as they were. Langston gave me the first song that I recited to my Sugar Hill thrill, that sweetie I made the "Harlem Love Poem" with, the poem I tried to memorize so that I could recite it to her when we sat on her project rooftop with all of Harlem in our hands.

RESETTLEMENT

John Ashbery

Here in the museum we do not invite trouble,
only establishment woes, sort of. We can bet farther
and classier with no returns. Sometimes late at night

cars droned and paled: Splurge and repent—
wasn't that the idea? It was your initiative
that brought us here, through the difficult part

of a city. Some angels
seemed to teeter on the wooden fence.
Were we all they knew?

Or are we part of their mind-cleansing
ritual, necessary and discardable?
Doesn't that make more sense?

Less than an hour before our return from the lake
the trees blossomed like shells exploding,
the landscape sucked in its breath,

taking its time as always.
I meant to speak to your mother about it,
but never forgave her for not being here, and drab,

the way mothers are supposed to be,
I think. Too many applications of the rule ensue.
There are too many, always with us

under the tree that stands on the lawn
but is no longer there, as if to prove it was a dream,
a different time slot.

CONTRIBUTORS

Chinua Achebe is a Nigerian novelist and poet. His books include *Things Fall Apart*, *A Man of the People*, and *Anthills of the Savannah*. He has received more than twenty honorary doctorates and several international literary prizes. A member of the American Academy and Institute of Arts and Letters, he teaches at Brown University.

Alison Anderson is a translator and the author of *Hidden Latitudes* and *Darwin's Wink*. She has translated the work of Amélie Nothomb, Sélim Nassib, and Muriel Barbery, among others. She received a National Endowment for the Arts Literary Translation Fellowship in 2004 and was a fellow for the EKEMEL House of Literature in Paros, Greece in 2005.

John Asfour is a Lebanese-Canadian translator and writer. He has published two volumes of poetry in Arabic and four in English, including *Fields of My Blood* and *Nisan*. He edited and translated the anthology *When the Words Burn: An Anthology of Modern Arabic Poetry*, which was shortlisted for the League of Poets Award.

John Ashbery has published more than twenty collections of poetry and won nearly every major award available to an American poet. His 1976 book *Self-Portrait in a Convex Mirror* won the National Book Award, the National Book Critics Circle Award, and the Pulitzer Prize. His most recent collections are *Notes from the Air* and *Planisphere*. He has also translated the work of many French writers; his translation of Rimbaud's *Illuminations* will be published next year.

Paul Auster is the author of *Invisible*, *The New York Trilogy*, *The Music of Chance*, and *Sunset Park*, which will be published later this year. He was a finalist for the 1991 PEN/Faulkner Award for Fiction and the recipient of the 2006 Prince of Asturias Award for Literature. He was elected to the American Academy of Arts and Letters in 2006.

Jesse Ball is the author of two novels, *Samedi the Deafness* and *The Way Through Doors*. A third, *A Ladder of Rain and the Roof Beyond*, will be published next year, along with *The Village on Horseback*, a collection of his poetry and prose. Ball received the Plimpton Prize in 2008. He teaches at the School of the Art Institute of Chicago.

Russell Banks was a finalist for both the Pulitzer Prize and the PEN/Faulkner Award in 1998 for his novel *Cloudsplitter*. An earlier novel, *Affliction*, was also a finalist for the PEN/Faulkner Award and was adapted into an award-winning film. The film adaptation of another book, *The Sweet Hereafter*, was nominated for two Academy Awards. Banks lives in upstate New York.

John Barth received the National Book Award for *Chimera* in 1972 and the PEN/Malamud Award for Excellence in Short Fiction in 1998. His books include *The Floating Opera, Lost in the Funhouse, Giles Goat-Boy, The Sot-Weed Factor*, and, most recently, *The Development*, a collection of stories set in a gated community in Maryland. He taught at Johns Hopkins University for many years before retiring from teaching in 1995.

Faraj Bayrakdar is a Syrian poet and journalist. In 1987, he was arrested on political charges. In 2000, after more than a decade in prison, and one year after he was named the recipient of the PEN/Barbara Goldsmith Freedom to Write Award, he was released with a presidential amnesty. He has published three collections of poems; *Mirror of Absences* was written while he was incarcerated.

Megan Mayhew Bergman grew up in North Carolina and now lives in Vermont. She has published stories in *Ploughshares, One Story, The Oxford American, The Kenyon Review, Shenandoah*, and elsewhere, and her work is featured in *New Stories from the South 2010*.

Daniel Brunet received a grant in 2010 from the PEN Translation Fund for his work on Dea Loher's play, *The Last Fire*. The 2003 Director in Residence at the English Theater Berlin, he has translated many plays and screenplays, including Heiner Müller's *Die Umsiedlerin*. He lives in Brooklyn and Berlin.

Lilli Carré is a cartoonist and animator based in Chicago. She has published several books, including *The Lagoon, Tales of Woodsman Pete*, and an illustrated adaptation of Hans Christian Andersen's *The Fir Tree*. Her work has been published in MOME, *Chicago Magazine*, GLÖMP, and elsewhere.

Michael Cunningham is the author of *By Nightfall, Specimen Days*, and *The Hours*, which won the Pulitzer Prize and the PEN/Faulkner Award in 1999. His work has been published in *The Atlantic Monthly, The Paris Review*, and many other publications. He teaches at Yale University.

Don DeLillo has published fifteen novels, including *Point Omega, Underworld, Libra*, and *White Noise*, which won the National Book Award in 1985. *Mao II* was nominated for the Pulitzer Prize for Fiction and received the 1991

PEN/Faulkner Award. He is the 2010 recipient of the PEN/Saul Bellow Award for Achievement in American Fiction.

Umberto Eco is an Italian philosopher, essayist, and novelist. His works include *The Mysterious Flame of Queen Loana*, *The Infinity of Lists*, and *The Name of the Rose*. He is president of the Scuola Superiore di Studi Umanistici at the University of Bologna, and an Honorary Fellow of Kellogg College at the University of Oxford. He lives in Milan.

Ezra E. Fitz is a translator focused on current Latin American literature. His previous translations, including *Shorts* by Alberto Fuguet and *The Obstacles* by Eloy Urroz, have been praised in *The New York Times*, *The New Yorker*, *The Believer*, and elsewhere. He was a 2010 Resident at the Banff International Literary Translation Centre in Alberta, Canada.

Peter Golub is a Moscow-born poet and translator. He is currently the translation consultant for the *St. Petersburg Review*. He received a grant in 2010 from the PEN Translation Fund and a Banff Centre Fellowship for his translation of Andrei Sen-Senkov's *Anatomical Theatre*, which will be published next year. He is a doctoral candidate at Columbia University.

Adam Gopnik has been writing for *The New Yorker* since 1986. He is the author of *Paris to the Moon*, *Through the Children's Gate*, *Angels and Ages*, and the children's book *The King in the Window*. He has won three National Magazine Awards for his essays and criticism, as well as a George Polk Award for Magazine Reporting.

Linor Goralik began working as a writer and journalist in the late '90s. Her novels include *No* (with Sergei Kuznetsov) and *Half of the Sky* (with Stanislav Lvovsky). She has also published *The Short Side of It*, a collection of flash fiction, as well as children's books, poetry, and translations. She received the Triumph Prize in 2003. She lives in Israel and Moscow.

Philip Gourevitch has written for *The New Yorker*, *Harper's*, *Granta*, and many other publications. From 2005 to earlier this year he was editor of *The Paris Review*. He received the National Book Critics Circle Award in 1998 for *We Wish to Inform You That Tomorrow We Will Be Killed with Our Families: Stories from Rwanda*. His most recent book is *The Ballad of Abu Ghraib*.

Marilyn Hacker is a poet and critic. Her work includes *Essays on Departure*, *Winter Numbers*, *Going Back to the River*, and *Presentation Piece*, which won the 1974 National Book Award. Her translation of Marie Étienne's *King of a Hundred Horsemen* won the 2009 PEN Award for Poetry in Translation, and she received the 2010 PEN/Voelcker Award for Poetry.

Jessica Hagedorn is a novelist, poet, playwright, and performance artist. Her novels include *Dream Jungle*, *The Gangster of Love*, and *Dogeaters*, which received the 1990 American Book Award and was a finalist for the National Book Award. Her work has been collected in *Stars Don't Stand Still in the Sky*, *Stage Presence*, *The Open Boat*, and elsewhere. She lives in New York.

Akinwumi Isola is a Nigerian playwright and poet who writes in both Yoruba and English. His wrote his first play, *Efunsetan Aniwura*, in the 1960s; many of his subsequent plays have been adapted for television and film. His first collection of poetry, *Afaimo and Other Poems*, is currently being translated into English.

Yusef Komunyakaa has published over a dozen books of poetry, among them *Warhorses*, *Pleasure Dome*, and *Neon Vernacular*, which received the 1994 Pulitzer Prize for Poetry as well as the Kingsley Tufts Poetry Award. He has also won a fellowship from the National Endowment for the Arts and the Ruth Lilly Poetry Prize. He teaches at New York University.

Inga Kuznetsova published her first poems at nineteen, winning the Pushkin National Prize for Student Poetry in 1995. Her first book of poems, *Sni-Sinitsi* (*Chickadee Dreams*), won the Triumph Prize and the Moscow Score Award for best debut in 2003. Her poems have been translated into English, French, Chinese, and Georgian.

Eduardo Lago is a novelist, translator, and critic whose books include *Llámame Brooklyn* (*Call Me Brooklyn*), which received the Nadal Prize, and *Ladrón de Mapas* (*Map Thief*). In 2002, he won the Bartolomé March Award for Excellence in Literary Criticism. He cofounded the Order of Finnegans and is currently director of the Instituto Cervantes in New York.

Anne Landsman was born and raised in South Africa. She won the 2009 South African *Sunday Times* Literary Award for her novel *The Rowing Lesson*. A previous novel, *The Devil's Chimney*, was a finalist for the PEN/Hemingway Award. She has written for *The Believer*, *Poets & Writers*, and many other publications. She lives in New York.

Jonathan Lethem has written several novels, including *Motherless Brooklyn*, which won the National Book Critics Circle Award; *The Fortress of Solitude*, a *New York Times* bestseller; and *Chronic City*. His newest book is *They Live*, a study of the eponymous film directed by John Carpenter. Lethem received a MacArthur Fellowship in 2005. He teaches at Pomona College.

Laura Lindstedt is a Finnish novelist, essayist, and critic. Her novel *Scissors* (*Sakset*), from which "and and and" is excerpted, was shortlisted for the 2007 Finlandia Award. She is the series editor of *Suomen kulttuurihistoria* (*A Cultural History of Finland*).

Dea Loher is a German playwright. Her awards include 2008 Mülheim Dramatists' Award for *The Last Fire*, the 2009 Berliner Literaturpreis, and the 2009 Marieluise Fleißer Preis. "Brightest Noon" is adapted from *The Last Fire*, which has not yet been published in English. Loher lives in Berlin.

Colum McCann is a novelist whose work has appeared in *The New Yorker*, *The Atlantic Monthly*, BOMB, and *The Paris Review*. His novels include *Dancer*, *Zoli*, and *Let the Great World Spin*, which received the National Book Award in 2009. He teaches at Hunter College and lives in New York.

Arthur Miller received the Pulitzer Prize for Drama, a George Foster Peabody Award, and a John F. Kennedy Lifetime Achievement Award, among many other honors. His plays include *Death of a Salesman*, *The Crucible*, *All My Sons*, and *After the Fall*. He served as Emeritus President of International PEN and Honorary Chair of PEN American Center before his death in 2005.

Albert Mobilio is an editor, critic, and poet whose books include *Me with Animal Towering*, *Letters from Mayhem*, and *A Handbook of Phrenology*. His work has appeared in *Harper's*, BOMB, *The Village Voice*, and elsewhere. He received a Whiting Writers' Award in 2000. He teaches at the New School in New York and co-edits *Bookforum*.

Quim Monzó was born in Barcelona in 1952 and reported from Vietnam, Cambodia, Northern Ireland, and East Africa in the early 1970s. He has since published several novels including *O'Clock*, *The Enormity of the Tragedy*, and *Gasoline*. He has also translated a number of English and American writers into Catalan.

Eshkol Nevo is an Israeli writer whose novels include *Osmosis* and *Homesick*, which received the Book Publishers Association Gold Prize and the Raymond Wallier Prize at the Salon du Livre. "Before the Next World Cup" is excerpted from his most recent novel, *World Cup Wishes*. Nevo teaches at the Sam Spiegel Film School, Tel Aviv University, and Sapir College.

Mary Ann Newman is director of the Catalan Center at New York University's Center for European and Mediterranean studies. She has translated Quim Monzó, Xavier Rubert de Ventós, Joan Maragall, Josep Carner, and Narcís Comadira, among others.

Amélie Nothomb was born to Belgian diplomats in Kobe, Japan. She has published many novels and story collections, including *The Character of Rain* and *Tokyo Fiancée*. *Fear and Trembling* won the Grand Prix du roman de l'Académie française in 1999. "The Art of Dealing with Geniuses" is adapted from *Hygiene of the Assassin*, which will be published later this year.

Akinloyé A. Òjó is a translator and a professor of comparative literature at the University of Georgia who focuses on Yoruba language and culture. He received a grant from the PEN Translation Fund in 2010 for his translation of *Afaimo and Other Poems* by Akinwumi Isola.

Stewart O'Nan is a novelist whose books include *Last Night at the Lobster*, *The Good Wife*, and *Songs for the Missing*. His novel *Snow Queen* was adapted into a film by David Gordon Green. *Granta* named him one of America's Best Young Novelists in 1996. His novel *Emily, Alone* will be published next year.

Willie Perdomo is a poet. His collection *Smoking Lovely* received a PEN Open Book Award in 2003. His other works include *Where a Nickel Costs a Dime*, *Postcards of El Barrio*, and the children's book *Visiting Langston*. The cofounder of Cypher Books, Perdomo teaches in New York City.

Helen Phillips has received a Rona Jaffe Writers' Award, the Italo Calvino Prize in Fabulist Fiction, and the Meridian Editors' Prize. Her stories have appeared in *The Mississippi Review*, *The Sonora Review*, and elsewhere. Her book *And Yet They Were Happy* will be published next year.

José Manuel Prieto is a Cuban novelist and translator. His novel *Nocturnal Butterflies of the Russian Empire* was published in English in 2002, and his novel *Rex* was a finalist for the 2010 Best Translated Book Award for Fiction. He teaches at Cornell University.

Atiq Rahimi is a writer and filmmaker who won the Prix Goncourt for his novel *The Patience Stone* in 2008. The film of his novel *Earth and Ashes* was an Official Selection at Cannes in 2004, and he is currently adapting his novel *A Thousand Rooms of Dreams and Fear* for the screen. He has set up a Writers' House in Kabul for young Afghan writers and filmmakers.

Arthur Rimbaud was a French poet. Born in 1854, he gave up writing before his twenty-first birthday. In 1873, he published *Une Saison en Enfer* as a small booklet in Brussels. "Lives" is a portion of his *Illuminations*, written in 1874 but not published until 1886. Rimbaud died in 1891.

Marilynne Robinson writes fiction and essays. Her first novel, *Housekeeping*, received the PEN/Hemingway Award, and her second, *Gilead*, received the Pulitzer Prize and the National Book Critics Circle Award. She published her third novel, *Home*, in 2008; her newest book, *Absence of Mind*, is a collection of essays. She teaches at the Iowa Writers' Workshop.

Daisy Rockwell (cover art) paints under the takhallus (or alias) "Lapata," an Urdu word for "missing" or "absconded." She was raised in a family of artists in western Massachusetts. She has a PhD in Hindi literature and contributes to the blog Chapati Mystery.

Lola Rogers is a translator of Finnish literature and a contributor to the magazine *Books from Finland*. Her translations include *Purge* by Sofi Oksanen, *The Sands of Sarasvati* by Petri Tolppanen and Jussi Kaakinen, and poetry by Eeva-Liisa Manner, published in *Female Voices of the North*.

Salman Rushdie is a former president of PEN American Center and the chair of the PEN World Voices Festival. His novels include *Midnight's Children*, *The Satanic Verses*, and *The Enchantress of Florence*. He has won the Booker Prize and two Whitbread Novel Awards and was knighted for services to literature in 2007. *Luka and the Fire of Life* will be published later this year.

Natalia Sannikova is a poet and journalist from the Sverdlovsk region of Russia. Her work has appeared in numerous literary journals and anthologies; her first book of poetry, *Intermezzo*, was published in 2003.

Saïd Sayrafiezadeh has published fiction and nonfiction in *The New Yorker*, *The Paris Review*, *Granta*, and many other publications. His memoir *When Skateboards Will Be Free* was selected as one of the ten best books of 2009 by *The New York Times*. He lives in New York.

Elissa Schappell is the author of *Use Me*, a finalist for the PEN/Hemingway Award, and the upcoming *Blueprints for Building Better Girls*. She co-edited the essay collections *The Friend Who Got Away* and *Money Changes Everything*. A contributing editor at *Vanity Fair*, Schappell was a co-founder of *Tin House*, where she is now Editor-at-Large. She teaches at New York University.

Deema Shehabi is a Palestinian-American poet and editor. Her work has appeared in *The Mississippi Review*, *Drunken Boat*, *The Kenyon Review*, and elsewhere, and she has been nominated for the Pushcart Prize. She lives in California and serves as the Vice President for the Radius of Arab-American Writers.

Sondra Silverston is a native New Yorker who has lived in Israel since 1970. Among her many published translations are works by Amos Oz, Etgar Keret, Eshkol Nevo, Savyon Liebrecht, and Aharon Megged.

Patti Smith is a writer, artist, and performer. Her albums include *Horses*, *Radio Ethiopia*, *Easter*, *Dream of Life*, *Gone Again*, and *Trampin'*. Her art retrospective, "Strange Messenger," has been exhibited around the world. Her books include *Witt*, *Babel*, *Woolgathering*, *The Coral Sea*, and *Just Kids*. In 2005, she was made a Commandeur de l'Ordre des Arts et des Lettres.

Andrzej Stasiuk is the author of several novels, including *Fado*, *Nine*, *Tales of Galicia*, and *White Raven*. He received the NIKE Award, Poland's most prestigious literary prize, for another book, *Going to Babadag*. Together with his wife, Stasiuk founded Wydawnictwo Czarne, a publishing house that specializes in Central and Eastern European authors.

Robert Stone received the National Book Award in 1974 for his novel *Dog Soldiers*. His 1981 novel *A Flag for Sunrise* won the PEN/Faulkner Award for Fiction. In 2007, he published a memoir, *Prime Green: Remembering the Sixties*. His most recent book is *Fun with Problems*, a collection of stories.

Lily Tuck is a novelist and writer of short stories. She received the National Book Award for her novel *The News from Paraguay*, and *Siam* was a finalist for the PEN/Faulkner Award. She has been published in *The New Yorker*, *Fiction*, *The Antioch Review*, and elsewhere. She lives in New York and Maine.

Eloy Urroz is a Mexican novelist and one of the authors of "The Crack Manifesto." His novel *The Obstacles* was published in English in 2006. "Probabilidad" is adapted from *Friction*, his most recent novel, which will be published in the United States later this year. Urroz teaches in South Carolina at the Citadel and the College of Charleston.

Matvei Yankelevich is a Russian-American poet and translator and the founding editor of Ugly Duckling Presse. He has published two volumes of poetry, *Boris by the Sea* and *The Present Work*, and translated the work of several Russian writers, including Daniil Kharms, Alexander Vvedensky, and Vladimir Mayakovsky.

Lila Azam Zanganeh is a writer and editor. A contributor to *Le Monde*, she has also written for *The New York Times*, *The Paris Review*, and *The International Herald Tribune*. She edited the collection *My Sister, Guard Your Veil; My Brother, Guard Your Eyes*, published in 2006, and her book *Nabokov, or The Invention of Happiness* will be published next year.

ACKNOWLEDGMENTS

"Frederick Douglass" by Robert Hayden was published in *Angle of Ascent*, copyright © 1975 by the estate of Robert Hayden.

"Admiration" and "The Decision" appeared in Catalan in *El perquè de tot plegat* by Quim Monzó. Copyright © 1993, 1999 by Joaquim Monzó and Quaderns Crema, S.A.U.

"Free Verses to My Son" by Natalia Sannikova, translated by Matvei Yankelevich. Translation copyright © 2010 CEC ArtsLink.

"Human Moments in World War III" by Don DeLillo originally appeared in *Esquire*, July 1983. Reprinted with the permission of the author.

"One Way to Disappear" by Lilli Carré first appeared as "Dorado Park" in *Nine Ways to Disappear*, copyright © 2009 by Lilli Carré. Little Otsu. Reprinted with the permission of the artist.

"Probabilidad" by Eloy Urroz, translated by Ezra E. Fitz, is excerpted from *Friction*, forthcoming from Dalkey Archive Press.

"Before the Next World Cup" by Eshkol Nevo is excerpted from *World Cup Wishes*. Copyright © by Eshkol Nevo. Published by arrangement with The Institute for the Translation of Hebrew Literature.